Deception of DISEASE

CHRISTA PROCTOR

Copyright © 2011 Impact Church Media

Impact Church
8330 Brady Lane
Roseville, CA 95747

www.impactchurch.info
www.deceptionofdisease.com
www.christaproctor.com

Deception of Disease
by Christa Proctor

ISBN 978-0-615-60226-4

Cover & Interior Design, Christa Proctor

Cover Photography, Snapped - Photography by Kim
www.snappedphotography.com

Unless otherwise indicated, Bible Quotations are taken from the King James Version. Copyright © 1979, 1980, 1982, Thomas Nelson, Inc., Publishers

For Danielle, Sophia, Victoria & Annalise
Your determination never ceases to amaze me.
Your future is so bright!

You have
nothing
to lose
by believing.

Contents

Preface/Disclaimer 7

1 Don't Ask, Don't Tell? What a Crock! 9

2 "There is No Autism" 21

3 When You Don't Know How To Do What 29

4 The Initial Results 39

5 What You Don't Know…*Can Kill* You. 49

6 Working The Inside-Out and The Outside-In 59

7 So How Is This Done? 65

8 Where Are They Now? 77

Supplemental 85

Acknowledgements 105

It's a situation that cannot be ignored.

Autism Prevalence Rates in the United States

1970's - 1 in every 10,000
1995 - 1 in every 1,000
1999 - 1 in every 500
2001 - 1 in every 250
2005 - 1 in every 166
2007 - 1 in every 150
2009 - 1 in every 91

Sources: The American Academy of Pediatrics and www.tacanow.org

"...the burden of proof is upon anybody who feels that there is NOT a real increase here in the number of kids affected."
Dr. Thomas Insel, Director of National Institute of Mental Health and head of Interagency Autism Coordinating Committee (IACC)

In 2009 a study conducted by the MIND Institute at UC Davis showed the increased autism rate in children from California was not due to better diagnosing. The MIND Institute found the autism increase to be genuine.

There is so much **you** can do.

Become *equipped* to encourage those who are groping in darkness.

There is *hope*.

There is *help*.

From those who have *overcome*...

Preface

A Mind Bending Idea
I used to think autism was the cause of quite mysterious and complex problems with which affected individuals would be faced throughout their lives. What I discovered is that autism doesn't cause anything. Rather, it's a mere label for a set of symptoms which CAN be traced to some root causes. Once the root issues are addressed, the deception of autism begins to unravel and the person who is affected is allowed to emerge.

If someone you love is affected by autism (or any type of PDD, ADD, ADHD, ODD, etc…) then the pages of this book will open your eyes to entirely new possibilities for their future. For your future together. A reformation is on the rise. We don't have to settle for managing symptoms and behaviors or coping with the situation forever. Things can change! But it starts inside. Give yourself permission to hope.

This book may not be for you. There may even be things I addressed in this book to which you are diametrically opposed. I don't pretend to be anything that I am not. Our experiences are not intended to be taken as advice (medical or otherwise) or an attempt to convert anyone over to our belief system or life strategies. I write only what we have seen, heard and experienced for ourselves, knowing it is but a snapshot of eternity, time and space. But I do it with the conviction that each voice <u>does</u> make a difference somewhere and to someone. Even if you and I don't agree, we can still be partners in global scale efforts. We can still inspire and encourage and accept one another unconditionally. We can also learn that when it comes right down to it, we will always have more in common than not. This is the spirit with which this book is presented, and I pray it's the spirit with which it's received. Whatever your journey, I wish you all the very best.

Disclaimer

The information contained in this book is not intended to dispense medical, legal or professional advice, nor does it prescribe any treatment or strategy that should be tested without the advice of a professional. Information presented in this book is for educational or entertainment purposes only. You are responsible for your own actions should you use any information found in this book.

1 Don't ask, don't tell? What a crock!

Sometimes the truth hurts. But wherever the truth is revealed, today's pain can be tomorrow's gain. And that's the way it is with autism.

By the time our family finally put a name with the face of what is called "Autism" my kids were 3 and 5 years old. Danielle had been in the system of special needs programs from the time she was 3, and Sophia had started even earlier at age 2. How did we not "get it" for two whole years? I became increasingly aware that the signs were there from the time I reached out for help, yet not even the professionals on our IEP team had the audacity to come right out and just tell us, in so many words, what we were actually dealing with. Here's what I mean...

Danielle's story:

She was a charming and beautiful baby, able to say about 10 words when she was seventeen months old. We took Danielle to Disney World that month, and she enjoyed everything right along with us. Then at around 18 months we noticed that she stopped speaking almost completely. She barely said a word over the next 12 months, except to request food. But talk about an easy child to have around! I remember taking her with us to 5 star restaurants and having her sit quietly in her chair or on our lap for the entire 3 hours.

When Danielle was around the age of 2 ½, I was fixing her hair in the bathroom one evening, and I was thrilled to hear her talking! As I tried to decipher the words coming from her mouth I began to realize that she was reciting dialogue from one of her favorite videos, the Veggie Tales. Her dad and I thought that was so cute and hoped she would soon use her speech to *dialogue with us*. As the weeks went on, however, we grew a bit more concerned about the possibility of a speech delay and decided to ask our doctor about it at the next well child appointment.

Our pediatrician was highly recommended and well-respected. At every check-up he had always seemed very interested in her overall development, but never seemed concerned about the fact that my answers to some of the developmental questions had been in the negative. Through time I have come to understand that I really can trust my gut feelings when it comes to my own children, but back then I made the assumption that the experts would recognize any problem (since they see it all the time), and that they would tell me about such problems without hesitation.

So when I brought up our concerns the doctor simply asked me, "Does she put two words together?"

"Sure," I said. There were lots of little phrases.

"thooz on" (shoes on)

"go sye" (go outside)

"mo peez" (more please)

What's more, she seemed to understand most of what we said to her. But there was so much I didn't even know to look for, like babble and back and forth exchanges of any type of communication, be it verbal or otherwise, not to mention the significance of things like eye contact or joint attention (pointing and saying, "Look at _____!"). When a child is typically developing, these things sort of "miraculously" fall into place. For instance how does a person learn that "me" and "you" do not refer to a specific person ("mommy hold you")? While most children sort of catch onto that concept, it can take *years* for a non typically developing child to really understand how personal pronouns are used. But when it's your first child and you don't know what to look for, you don't miss what you've never had. You don't even know what you don't know.

The doctor felt that we should give it time and recommended that we talk about it again in 6 months at her 3 year old check-up. Big mistake. Fortunately we acted on instinct and called our county's Infant Program to request an assessment of our child's speech. She was now 5 weeks away from her 3rd birthday and I was nervous about letting "some government agency" come in and possibly assert any sort of agenda upon my family. How pleasantly surprised I was when some absolutely wonderful people came into our home to help discover potential deficits that were affecting our child.

When the assessment report came back, her abilities and deficits were all there in black and white. But when you don't even know what you're looking for, you are simply taking it all in as raw data. Most of the report explained that her expressive language, fine motor, cognition (I had never used this word in conversation before and even had to ask the meaning), and social emotional development were all at about the 24-28 month age range, which in my mind simply confirmed what I suspected. That she was about a year behind in some things – a late bloomer. I figured she'd probably catch up fine with a little bit of help. No one used any words that I can remember such as "developmentally delayed," "special needs," and definitely no one even hinted at the possibility of Autism or any other PDD (Pervasive Developmental Disorder).

I think a lot of assumptions were probably made by those assessing my child about my ability to interpret the findings and just "put 2 & 2" together.

I wish someone had gone ahead and spelled it all out for me, not afraid of insulting my intelligence. Not just reporting evidence of what I *already* knew about my child, but going on to explain in detail the potential ramifications of all the data, based on their vast experience in working with all types of children. And now that I am intimately familiar with all the terms that were presented in that report, my feeling is that a glossary of terms would have also benefited me tremendously. How did I know that certain phrases in such reports contain way more meaning than meets the eye? Inherent in their meaning is a bundle full of implications. To me, terms like "least restrictive environment" and "organizing information" meant simply what they said. The reality is that these are not simple phrases or figures of speech, but rather complete subject headings about which entire books can be written. But again, not even aware of the existence of this type of knowledge, I did not request more in depth explanations and readily accepted the recommendation to provide her with speech therapy and then enroll her that fall into a speech class.

It was a relief to have a team of experts working with us (Special Education representative, Child Psychologist, Speech & Language Pathologist, School District and County Office of Education representatives, teachers, etc.). All these individuals were genuinely great people who cared about understanding the needs of my child. So I relaxed a bit inside feeling confident that they would tell me whenever they thought something different needed to be done with or for her. Once we got through the first month of tears, Danielle seemed to really enjoy her new class which met for about 1 1/2 hrs three times each week. But after being a helper in this great class, it didn't take very long for me to wonder how this environment was really addressing my child's needs. It was not any more intensive that what she was offered in her Sunday School classroom each week, which certainly was not specifically targeting speech and language – so how was this addressing her needs? When I asked her school teacher what she thought about it, I noticed the eagerness in her eyes as she said, "Are you thinking about asking for an IEP?"

"Do you think I should?"

"Yes, if you have any thoughts that this is not the right placement for her, then you should."

"Well, I guess so. So, I'm the one that calls these meetings? I thought that you guys would be the ones to tell *me* if it's needed."

"The parents can request an IEP at any time. I'll turn in the forms right away. And would you allow me to request an evaluation by the school psychologist?"

"Sure, if you think that's necessary."

As soon as I broached the subject, the sense of urgency immediately emerged from this teacher's demeanor. *If she was as concerned as I am that Danielle's needs are not being addressed, then why hadn't she already brought this up to me? After all, these people are the ones who have experience in these matters.* That is when it hit me…I'm the one that has to bring up the concerns in order for them to be addressed. And the sad fact is that for me it was all uncharted territory. I began to feel as if I had to grope in the dark, while those I had leaned on to guide me were just watching me from the light, waiting to act on our behalf only if and when I happened to find a door to knock on.

As the weeks progressed, the psychological assessment was complete, and we found ourselves around the little table in Danielle's classroom, seated across most of the very same people who had been in my home not one year prior. The ones that, until now, I thought had so skillfully guided us thus far. By the end of our time together, we had received a report that Danielle presented "autistic-like-behaviors." The new recommendation was to move her into a class for children on the autistic spectrum.

Let me pause here to say that my husband and I are not prone to worry about things. For example if I get a headache my mind does not wander off to thoughts of a brain tumor. When I was pregnant there was a very popular book that I bought so that I could read about what to expect during my pregnancy. I actually discarded it after about the 4th month because in my opinion it should have been named, "Everything that Can Possibly go Wrong During Your Pregnancy." If something bad happens we deal with it head on, but we don't like to waste energy thinking about things that will probably never happen. We are people who mentally and conversationally rehearse the best case scenario in any of life's events, and we have found that it's been highly profitable to take most things at face value or even with just a grain of salt.

Moreover, the little I knew about Autism had convinced me that almost every person on the planet has some "autistic-like" behaviors. So we interpreted this news to mean that there were simply a few behaviors that, if addressed, would not hinder our child's development or education in any way. *I mean, if it was actual Autism that we needed to be concerned about, they would have said that, right?* But no, we were just dealing with some "autistic-like behaviors." For this reason I felt relieved that a little time in this new class would help address those behaviors until she was ready for a "regular" class (whatever *that* is, by the way).

You would think that Autism is something like bad breath or body odor. You know how something is obvious to everyone else but they're afraid of hurting your feelings or disappointing you so they don't say anything?

Danielle really gained some great academic skills during her first year in the new ASD (Autism Spectrum Disorder) class. As she began her second year in there (now Kindergarten), we were still optimistic but wondered why we weren't getting a handle on some of these behaviors. Maybe we weren't the amazing parents we always believed we would be, so we took advantage of some great parenting classes in order to help us raise a happier and more compliant child.

In the meantime our second daughter, Sophia, had also exhibited quite a language delay and not wanting to make the same mistakes again, we wasted no time in getting her assessed and took advantage of the recommended in-home speech and language therapy. When Sophia turned 3 it was now time for the school district to take over providing for her speech services. As I investigated what they had to offer at the time, I could not find the kind of happy environment I wanted for my child. I thought about the wonderful program that Danielle was in, but that was offered by the county - not the district, and I wondered how I could get Sophia in that class. I still understood so little about Autism. At that point I was just following my gut in resisting her being placed in the classes being offered. I knew Danielle's program was a better fit even though I didn't realize Sophia was on the Autism Spectrum. I began to wonder if Sophia also had some "Autistic-like Behaviors" that I was overlooking.

When I brought this up to her speech therapist, I thought I was experiencing déjà vu. I perceived the same eager demeanor I had encountered just over a year ago with Danielle's teacher. It was astonishing to realize that once again, they were watching and waiting to see if I would stumble onto the facts they had seen so clearly from the beginning. Once we began the new assessment process for school placement, there were so many "autistic-like" behaviors revealed that I now wondered about my qualifications as a mother. Sophia's behaviors were very different from Danielle's, and not knowing what to look for nor having a typically developmental point of reference, I had again missed what was so obvious to the experts (who I was still trusting to spell it all out for me).

Suddenly the information I had slowly and painstakingly acquired while trying to raise now 3 daughters (by this time, we had a third daughter, Victoria) started adding up inside. It all pointed not to some peculiar behaviors that could be addressed externally, but to a systemic problem that the world calls Autism.

"That's what this is? We're not just clueless parents who can't even get their kids interested in playing with us? Why didn't anyone just point it out in the first place?"

When I later expressed these sentiments to our regional center special services coordinator, she explained that it's very hard to tell parents this in such plain terms. Many times parents get offended or hurt, or they just don't believe it. My reply to her was that if medical doctors used that logic, they would never give you a diagnosis. How would you like to walk around with cancer & not know it because your doctor didn't want to upset you?

We were concerned enough when Danielle was only 3 years old to invite total strangers into our home, weren't we? Why? So they could report on the raw data they had received from our own mouths in the first place? We already knew the data...we were living that part. We had wanted to understand, from their expert opinion, the reasons behind it all.

So now it was a time for grace and forgiveness on our part. Of course, these people may not have realized back when we first reached out for help, how in the dark about all this we really were. But assumption is the lowest form of knowledge, and there were plenty of assumptions made on both sides of the coin. We felt as if years had been taken from us. Countless and precious opportunities for early intervention now lost. But at least now we knew what we were dealing with. And deal with it, we would.

CHRISTA PROCTOR

JUST SO YOU KNOW...
Here are a just few of the signs our children exhibited. (Though we saw these things, we didn't know they were potentially "symptoms" of anything.)

Danielle - Age 5	Sophia - Age 3
Lack of eye contact	Hand flapping
Severe Speech Delay	Severe Speech Delay
Severe Language Delay	Severe Language Delay

Note: we didn't know the difference between "speech" and "language" and we also thought they would just "grow out of it" – that they were simply late talkers.

Fixations on certain toys	Would not play with toys except to line up specific & related groups of toys
Lined things up all the time	
Scripting *(Ability to memorize large portions of movies was her main form of talking.)*	Communicated only with grunts
Refused to play with us	Refused to play with us Could not ask or answer, "What's that?"
Extreme Stubbornness	**Extreme** Stubbornness
Non age-appropriate tantrums	Constantly picked at her skin, *creating* scabs
Extreme pickiness about everything	Non-interest in social interaction

Danielle - Age 5	Sophia - Age 3
Inability to pretend play with kids	No joint attention
Echolalia *(repeating every word spoken to her)*	Could not answer "yes" or "no" questions
Obsessive Compulsive Behaviors	
Developmental Age: Communication - 2.5yrs Daily Living Skills - 3.5 yrs	Developmental Age: Communication - 1 yr Daily Living/Relationship Skills - 9 mo.

There was so much more, but these are a few of the things we chalked up to our being inept parents.

CHRISTA PROCTOR

2 "There Is No Autism"

Do you know what it's like to not want to go to sleep at night, because you're not sure you can face the challenges that await you in the morning? I'm sure many who are reading this do. And I'm not talking about a few weeks, but rather month after month (and into the years for some). Let me tell you the story about how all that changed for us.

Once we realized what we were actually dealing with, a whole new gamut of guilt and other emotions were unleashed. First we felt tremendously grieved over having misunderstood the very heart and intent of our children's behaviors. There was guilt over how we had disciplined them for things beyond their control, now seeing that their seeming unwillingness to comply with the simplest of requests was mostly not a matter of "I won't," but rather, "I can't," or more accurately, "I can't process my environment, let alone what you are telling me."

Then, there were heightened sensitivities on our part toward the thoughts or remarks of others (even our loving family) who simply could not fathom the degree of what we were really dealing with at the time. Whether imagined or real, we perceived that some people ignorantly and innocently wondered what the big deal was. I sort of felt that people were thinking that *all kids have their difficulties*, and that maybe they thought we were reading into things or trying to see things that weren't there. I probably felt this because it's a judgment I had previously passed toward so many other parents in my short life.

Christmas was fast approaching and the obsessive compulsive behaviors which began only months prior, had become so severe in Danielle that we were now all prisoners in our own home. She was being controlled by this evil thing, and that control was extending its rule to every facet of our home life. The tasks of dressing, handing her a plate of food, shutting her car door, giving her any kind of affection, literally anything physically or socially related to her, would have to be done over and over, and in just the right sequence (which was impossible to figure out at times). I remember feeling so relieved when she finally got out the door and on the bus in the mornings. It was a brief reprieve each day from this terrible thing that was making what tiny bit of communication we did have even more difficult.

Hours upon hours would be spent among a team of people (teachers, psychologists, speech pathologists, behaviorists, etc.) to strategize the best way to avoid and deal with each of the behaviors. Once a plan was implemented then new triggers would set off a new behavior. You could jump through one hoop, but then there were five new ones waiting to blindside you.

I won't even go into all the details. First, if you are not experiencing Autism and its accompanying symptoms in your own home, as close as you may be to the family, you simply would not even be able to imagine it. This is not a slam by any means. Likewise I'm sure that I would not be able to imagine your own personal struggles unless I have walked in them myself. We can have empathy for one another, and we can choose not to make a judgment of one another, and that kind of human compassion is enough for us to really accept each other and get along well. Second, if you *are* experiencing this, then you need no further explanation or gory details. And for your benefit there are other books which can help you better understand the disorder and where your child is coming from.

Suffice it to say, Christmas that year had culminated into the darkest season of our lives. Due to lack of information about the nature of this problem, there were still typically reasonable expectations by loved ones in place for these beautiful children who were now 3 and 5. There were expectations for them to act a certain way on Christmas (happy) and to want to play with their new gifts (or at least want to open them). Expectations which we, as parents, now knew were totally unrealistic for the time being, and it put a great deal of strain upon us as a family. The ability to enjoy typical things in a typical fashion had literally vanished from our children right under our noses. And having just understood the diagnosis ourselves, the deficits were now glaringly obvious to us for what they were and it was just the saddest and most difficult thing I've ever had to face in my life.

All of that to say, it was plain hard to know which end was up. But this one thing we knew for sure: God had not planned this for our children. It was not by His design. The Bible is very clear that He does not appoint anyone to torment, confusion, or lack of any kind. We have always believed this and taught this, and we took this as another opportunity to trust in God and His good character. The Bible is true when it says, "Many are the afflictions of the righteous, BUT the Lord DELIVERS him OUT of them ALL." Back when we thought it was a parenting issue, we did all we could to do our part. Now that we were "lost" we ran to the only One who could show us what to do. "If any of you lacks wisdom, let him ask of God, who gives to all liberally and without reproach, and it will be given to him." James 1:15

Let me say here that although I would love for everyone, everywhere to know God personally through believing in Jesus Christ, my purpose here is not to convince you of His presence or to convert you to Christianity. However, FAITH, pure and simple, is being sure of what you cannot see. And that, my friend, is a requirement for anyone who would dare to outlast any of life's storms! You simply must believe that you will overcome. That your child will overcome.

Although we knew not how, we were SURE that our girls would end up completely free from every bondage or symptom of Autism. (The definition of faith is being confident of what you hope for yet cannot see with your natural eyes.) It was interesting for me to initially discover among the "Autism Community" two very different approaches toward this diagnosis. One approach is to completely embrace the diagnosis, believing it to be a gift, and to base one's identity, lifestyle, and life goals upon it. The other was to see it as something to be overcome or fought. We definitely considered ourselves in the second category.

That first week of January in 2006, just following that dark Christmas, my husband and I embarked on a prolonged time of fasting and prayer. We also scheduled appointments for our girls to be prayed for by other persons who specialized in ministry to children. We wanted to address this from every possible angle: spiritually, emotionally, and physically. We prayed in faith, knowing that God would show us the way of abundant life and health. It felt like a full court press, or like we were in a boxing match and were hitting our invisible opponent over and over and over again in the head, determined not to quit until he was down for the count.

During the third week of January we attended an annual conference with pastors from the Northern California area. These are dear friends that have prayed and encouraged each other through some very good and very hard times. Among the gathering were people with gifts of healing, meaning that when they pray for the sick miracles regularly take place. Using the Apostle Paul's example in the Bible, we took cloths, put oil on them, and had these friends lay hands on the cloths and pray for the healing of our girls. These cloths would later be placed under their bed sheets.

I remember that night well, as I cried out to God from the very depths of my soul, thanking Him for hope and telling Him that I refused to be denied. Not that I thought He was withholding anything, but more to the point that everything within me was taking a stand upon His promises, determined not to be moved one bit from my faith and confidence in Him, knowing that everything in life will work out for our good. I knew we would come out of this thing on top, no matter how long it took, because we trust in God. And every single thing will play into His hands if we have faith in Him to rescue us.

That very next Saturday I went to an appointment I had previously made with a long-time doctor friend of ours. Among all the special education, behavioral therapy, and other services we were incorporating into our lives, we thought we would also check into the possibility of heavy metal toxicity, so our plan was to go over the results of a simple hair analysis. The first thing she pointed out was that little to no mercury was showing up in either of the girls' hair. What that means is that the heavy metals were not escaping the body. It actually signified an underlying problem.

"What are you currently doing for them?" she asked.

"Well, they are in really great schools, and we are now on a waiting list for in-home programs, and…"

"No, no, no. All that's fine and all, but it's really not going to address the problem."

My mind began to race. *Ok, so she obviously knows something that I don't. And she's so confident about it. So, is this about the shots?* Friends of ours had a terrible experience about 2 weeks after their daughter received vaccines at 6 months of age. Her life was in danger and she was having severe seizures. They found a holistic doctor that helped her completely recover in about 2 years, and they mentioned that the same protocols were often used to treat kids with Autism. But our kids didn't show such immediate and severe reactions to their shots, so we never necessarily linked their problems to that.

As I relayed this story to the doctor, she validated the theory that we needed to address this physiologically. She and her husband recommended a website to me called "Generation Rescue." As soon as I got home, I began to devour every word on the site. My eyes were opened to an entirely new world of people who had overcome this thing that attempts to silence and steal our children. I was in touch every day with other parents looking for ways to help their kids. How was it possible that no one had yet clued me into this stuff?

The next day was Sunday, and as my husband was preaching at church, I heard the words very clearly in my mind, "There is no Autism."

I thought, *"That's right, I believe that, Lord! I can see there being no such thing as Autism in our home and in the lives of my girls."*

To me it was a faith-filled thought, you know, believing in what you cannot see? Well, that night I continued to read the astounding information on the generationrescue.org site, and the last page I saw said this:

Old Paradigm:

Mercury may or may not be one of the causes of Autism. Once you have Autism, it is lifelong. Autism is genetic. Treatment is behavioral therapy with a psychologist or a social worker. Prognosis for recovery is very poor.

New Paradigm:

Mercury causes mercury poisoning, which has been mislabeled as Autism. Mercury poisoning can be resolved by removing the mercury. Mercury poisoning is an issue of toxicology. Treatment is the removal of mercury through a process called chelation. Prognosis for recovery is very good.

And then I remembered the words I believed God had said to me while at church. "THERE IS NO AUTISM."

CHRISTA PROCTOR

3 When You Don't Know How to do What

When an entire new world is opened up to you for the first time, you honestly don't know how you can possibly take it all in. Where do you start looking? What if you explore down a road you think looks good, only to realize later you should have turned the other way? The world of Autism recovery is so vast that once you discover it you wonder how it could ever have been hidden from you in the first place. And even more mystifying is that most of the families affected by Autism are somewhat familiar with a few of the treatments which have produced success, but there are very few who actually put it all to work in any kind of substantial way.

I had heard of some of my kids' classmates being on special diets, but was told they really only helped kids who had digestive problems. I had also heard of chelation therapy and at first thought that was supposed to be THE magic bullet. Get the metal out and boom, you've got your child back. Then I went to a biomedical forum and heard about something called an oxygen chamber. I didn't have much knowledge, but I had heard of something else called the DAN (Defeat Autism Now) website and immediately began contacting every DAN Doctor within 50 miles. This was a disappointing endeavor when I realized I was more aware of current biomedical protocols than the ones many of them employed for treating children with the diagnosis.

There were two world-class holistic doctors we had heard about. It was exciting to speak with families who had been treated by these doctors and had seen their children recover. What we learned was that it is very important to find a doctor who has a proven track record. You will not, by the way, even be told that recovery is possible by most allopathic physicians.

Western medicine is so wonderful for treating acute symptoms. If my child had a broken leg or was in a car accident, I would take them to the ER without question and be thankful for the technology and lifesaving medication & methods. But for any type of chronic disease or illness, I quickly came to understand that a more holistic approach is vital.

Our journey to choose a doctor presented quite a few challenges to our theology at the time. The more I investigated successful medical protocols, the more I heard about methods that I had always attributed to Eastern Religion. Eastern Religions often contain many thoughts and philosophies that are contrary to our personal Judeo Christian beliefs, so this seemed to threaten our pursuit of a successful doctor. Interestingly enough, one of the specialists we were considering was a born-again Christian who employed some of these techniques we had always thought to be taboo (literally).

One night after we had really been seeking God's prescription for our daughters' journey to health, God again spoke to me. What He said was simply this, "Luke was an Eastern Physician." Luke was a close friend and disciple of Jesus and one of the original twelve apostles in the early Christian church. In those days the "West" did not exist as we know it. So we began to pray that God would help us discern the difference between Eastern Medicine and Eastern Religion. Let me try and explain. I wanted to know if there were any truths I had rejected simply because they were shared by an un-Christian religion. If someone who worships a god I do not serve, can teach me to understand vital truth that will help me, then being enlightened by them does not mean I am embracing the god they serve, as long as the enlightenment can be supported by Scripture (the Word of God). Historically many religions other than Christianity have been much more open to incorporating laws of physics and biology into their study of truth. Fortunately, that is changing.

The Earth is the Lord's and everything in it, including science, energy, laws of physics, and all kinds of proven ancient medical technology. But we all tend to be uncomfortable with the unknown. So we did not want to base our decision on religion, but rather our trust in the unfailing wisdom of our Father-Creator. The Bible was our litmus test. We decided to proceed with this Christian doctor and would test everything against the Bible. If we found anything that did not align with the teachings of Christ we would simply back out of the situation and pray for God to show us a new door.

We were absolutely thrilled about embarking on the journey to get our girls back. I remember telling my mom once that I felt like Danielle was growing up but we weren't getting the joy and privilege of actually knowing her. Sure, we knew her and loved every moment of life with her. But we wanted to know what was on her mind. What did she think about various things? Her friends? Her opinions, likes and dislikes? There were enough glimpses into her so we could tell she had a compassionate heart and that she was smart and had a great sense of humor. But it would grieve us to think about the fact that we had never had one conversation with our beautiful 5 year old girl. And our 3 year old could say only mommy and daddy but would otherwise just grunt and point.

It gave us such hope and determination to realize that we were not dealing with some mystical disorder. They were simply physically sick in some way. And we knew in our hearts that if we could provide their bodies with the proper nutrients and safe environment, the natural healing process would be able to work for them.

What would this journey hold for us? I interviewed a mother who lived 7 hours away from me. She had taken her son to the same doctor we were considering a couple of years prior and her son was now almost symptom free. I took copious notes on everything she did for him. I wrote down all the foods she fed him, down to the brand names as well as the name of a cookbook she recommended. I understood almost nothing she was telling me. It would make sense for a moment, but as soon as our hour & a half phone conversation ended the comprehension seemed to vanish. It was like taking a lesson from a teacher who spoke a foreign language. She talked as if it was all second nature to her, and I wondered if I would ever be able to get a handle on it.

The number one question I had for her at the end was, "So what do I do right now?" Her answer brought me right back to the beginning. She said, "What you do is you pray to God every single day and you ask Him to show you exactly what you need to do for your girls." And that was exactly right. There are no pat answers in life. Only God knows how to untie every single knot. Each one has its own twists and turns and process through which it became entangled. He understands all that seems mysterious to us and is happy to reveal it to His children when we ask. Step by step.

During part of the conversation she mentioned that some of the treatments were based upon the principles of quantum physics. I noted that and thought I would try and look up a simple explanation for the meaning of this on the internet later that day. Ha! Now that's comical in and of itself. I won't go into all I've learned about this subject (which isn't a whole lot anyway), but I will say that it's one of the most exciting studies

I've ever done. Intimidating, yes. With a field full of scientists who have turned to all kinds of spiritual teachings (Christianity being one) because they find scientific evidence of spiritual realms, to me it's a wonderful and beautiful science that theoretically proves the teachings of Christ and the Apostles. All of the science actually verifies faith and scriptural truth. As we discovered this, we became even more convinced that we were on an exciting new adventure which combined God's beautiful faith and science.

Of course, why wouldn't there be methods and techniques that God designed which would combine spiritual, emotional, and physical elements? Quantum physics helped me to understand that everything in life that we consider physical and material is actually made up of spiritual properties. When you get down to the sub-atomic level of any type of matter (a table, for instance), you will find that there is more space than there are particles of matter. The smaller the particles are, they seem not to consistently occupy the same place in time and space. All matter is simply made up of particles which vibrate at various frequencies in order to manifest as matter in the physical dimensions of time and space. Everything is made up of energy (or sound waves), as are you and I. Everything is from Him and exists by His Spirit, and that includes what we see in the physical realm. Whenever Jesus teaches us how things that are seen are subject to the things that are unseen, and that we have authority over physical matter, we should be taking this literally.

> Matthew 17:20 So Jesus said to them, "...for assuredly, I say to you, if you have faith as a mustard seed, you will say to this mountain, 'Move from here to there,' and it will move; and nothing will be impossible for you.

> Matthew 21:18-21 Now in the morning, as He returned to the city, He was hungry. And seeing a fig tree by the road, He came to it and found nothing on it but leaves, and said to it, "Let no fruit grow on you ever again." Immediately the fig tree withered away. And when the disciples saw it, they marveled, saying, "How did the fig tree wither away so soon?" So Jesus answered and said to them, "Assuredly, I say to you, if you have faith and do not doubt, you will not only do what was done to the fig tree, but also if you say to this mountain, 'Be removed and be cast into the sea,' it will be done."
>
> Luke 17:6 So the Lord said, "If you have faith as a mustard seed, you can say to this mulberry tree, 'Be pulled up by the roots and be planted in the sea,' and it would obey you."

Our trip to the doctor entailed booking flights, a rental house for a week, an initial consultation at $300/hour, and a series of laser therapy detoxification treatments during each day that we were there. This was an expensive endeavor. None of which would be covered by insurance (in *my* opinion insurance companies are not into prevention or cure – just treatment of symptoms). Our wonderful friends and family believed so much in what we were doing that they came out of the woodwork to help us financially. Not only that, but they started a daily prayer vigil to align their faith with ours during the entire week.

We arrived at the vacation rental home late at night and looked forward to getting the kids settled right into bed. There were 7 of us all together because my parents had come along to help, since none of us knew for sure the type of work we would be doing that week. Upon entering the house we were shocked to find eastern religious idols and large posters of Buddhist monks in every room of the house. Danielle was extremely disturbed by the images and idols and had strong emotional outbursts over the items. She would not be calmed down until we very carefully removed all of the religious artifacts and placed them safely in the garage. We wanted to be careful with the property since it did not belong to us, and we were certain that it held special meaning to the owner. But we took this as a sign that our enemy, the devil, was trying to find any entrance possible into the situation to distract us. We cleansed the atmosphere of the house with much prayer and we all had a good night's sleep.

On the day of our first consultation we were so happy to meet the kind and compassionate doctor. We fell in love with him, and our kids did too. Little did we know that our lives were in for major restructuring. Every way of life for us would be subject to change, and we had no clue as to what we were actually getting ourselves into. He examined each girl for an hour and a half. The entire process was absolutely painless and easy. It was all done through assessing their energy patterns (frequencies) and determining what types of foods and toxins needed to be eliminated from their system and then avoided. In addition, specific nutritional and herbal protocols were written according to each child's needs. We left the office that day with a small book of customized things "to-do" every hour of every day for the coming year. And it would all start the next morning, prior to the first detox treatment.

Now, there is more than one way to detoxify your body. There may be some who, like me, thought that detox was only for people addicted to alcohol or drugs. The specific therapy the girls received was invented by the very doctor we were seeing, and he actually trains other doctors in these same procedures. We've always prayed for the best of everything for our girls, and that's why we were glad we found him. We were actually referred to him by our doctor friend I talked about in the previous chapter. Anyway, his method of detoxification is a rapid laser energy therapy. It looks like something out of Star Trek as the laser beam is directed over their palms, the bottoms of their feet, as well as other inflamed areas such as the brain, etc. Each toxin has a corresponding (or resonating frequency) remedy that is specific to each individual. (This is where the principles of quantum physics come into play.)

So, on the first day they were detoxed from sulfites. For the next 25 hours they could not come into contact with any food or chemical that contained sulfites (even certain brands of bottled water). What was a real challenge was the day they were detoxified from plastic. Try not touching plastic for even 1 hour, let alone 25 (think about it). We quarantined them that day in the master bedroom and put medical gauze and cloth tape over all of the light switches, toilet seat, etc. They were CHAMPS! For the entire 7 days they could not touch anything electrical or be in the room with someone using a cell phone. The electromagnetic frequencies of any electronic device (including a TV remote, etc.) would potentially disrupt the effects of the therapy. Throughout our stay they were also detoxed from herbicides/pesticides, heavy metals, and a couple of other groups of toxins that were affecting them. Again, each person is different, but my feeling now is that all of us on planet Earth could benefit from detox of all the above.

He recommended that we take the entire list of supplements, herbs, and homeopathic remedies that he had written up, and that we pray over it as a family. We appreciated the fact that he admitted he's only human and that we should ask God to show us if there is anything that would not be right for our girls. We can run the risk, if we're not careful, of turning anything into bondage – even a medical protocol from a world renowned doctor. Although we were thankful to find this new path, we had to remember that it's God who is our Healer and our Source of answers.

CHRISTA PROCTOR

4 THE INITIAL RESULTS

This is what many of us want to know. Is there something out there that really works? Can our kids become free from the physiological damage that keeps them locked inside of their own bodies? What's the bottom line?

The first sign of the detox having an effect was actually during the second day of treatments while we were in the rental house. I was holding our 3 year old, Sophia, and was rubbing her back and tummy just to love on her. The surprise at what I felt was so overwhelming that I had to raise up her shirt to take a look at her torso. For months she had very rough small bumps (like sandpaper) all over her torso and arms. But now, her skin was as smooth as could be. When I raised up her shirt to take a look I could see traces and red blotches where the bumps and patches had been, but the skin itself was completely smooth! Something was definitely happening inside that little body of hers.

Day number 3 was the day they were detoxed from plastics, and the day we quarantined them into one bedroom for the entire 25 hours. We placed a portable DVD player up really high on some furniture so that they could not possibly come in contact with it and we would take snacks and meals in to them. During one of the times I was delivering a snack, I noticed they were having a back and forth exchange of communication with one another for the first time EVER. Danielle was mumbling some sort of vocalization (attempt at words I think), and Sophia would repeat it, and then they laughed together. They did this together about 5-10 times, like they were "joking around" together. I was astonished. They were "sharing a moment" and laughing together. It was a huge breakthrough and another sign that there really was something to this detox thing.

We made it through that initial week of LED treatments, and then flew home to California. I remember hour after hour, day after day, week after week of diligently following the instructions. And the weeks turned into months. So many of the supplements were homeopathic herbs and flower remedies. Some that were administered orally, but others that we rubbed on their tummies. One day these thoughts kept running through my mind like, "We spent all this money for remedies as simple as drops of water?" I'll never forget it because I happened to be in the shower thinking about this.

Immediately God brought the passage of scripture to my mind about a man named Naaman who had leprosy. In his day it was the worst kind of incurable disease. He was a wealthy and influential man. He and his entourage traveled a far distance to see a prophet of God in order to obtain healing. When the prophet told him what he must do to be healed he became very disappointed and even angry about it. You see, the instructions were for him to go wash himself seven times in the Jordan River and his skin would be cleansed of the disease. He was looking for something spectacular to do.

His servants were so level-headed and wise about the whole matter. They basically said to him, "If the prophet had told you to do some grand and difficult thing, wouldn't you have done it? All the more reason for you to do something as simple as this." So he went down and dipped himself in the Jordan seven times as the man of God had told him, and his flesh was restored and became clean like that of a young boy. (2 Kings 5:1-13) This event actually occurred. It's not a parable.

After that I understood that with God sometimes the most dramatic results come through seemingly simple and ordinary means. We faithfully stuck to the protocols, through good days and bad. Let me share with you the actual Christmas Letter that we sent to our friends and family at the end of that year. This will give you a snapshot into how many amazing changes we experienced in a short time...

OUR MIRACLE YEAR
DECEMBER 2006 - CHRISTMAS LETTER

Exactly one year ago, during our annual Christmas photo shoot, 195 candid photos were taken but we were only able to get one shot of us all looking toward the camera at the same time. We still got some beautiful pictures of the girls, but this experience was yet another reminder that our two oldest daughters were fading away from us and had withdrawn into their own world – one which we found to be virtually inaccessible. We could rarely get them to play with us or even allow us to join in their isolated play. We had never had a conversation with Danielle at this point, and she was 5 ½ years old. Sophia only communicated through grunts and had just been diagnosed with Autism (age 3). She did not even point her finger in order to reference things or people.

Refusing to accept the nightmarish prognosis for our daughters, we decided to declare war on this horrible disorder that was trying to literally overtake our household and steal our children. Confident through the Word of God that this was not God's will for our daughters, we went into intense battle with this enemy. Through much prayer and fasting in January, we experienced a breakthrough of knowledge and guidance from our good and faithful God, resulting in a customized detoxification protocol which began in March when the Lord directed us to a specialist in Phoenix, Arizona. Family and friends gathered around us in astounding ways through prayer and even financial assistance in order for this to happen.

Here are some of Christa's journal entries from the past year…

May 2006
Danielle has already begun saying some spontaneous sentences here and there. For example, instead of saying "No going outside!" or "No outside!" she says, "I don't want to go outside." We are blown away by these things. She used to only speak scripted comments she had learned from videos. Neither of them will yet engage with a camera.

June 7, 2006
A long time ago I stopped bothering to ask the girls to look at or smile at the camera. It seems a lost cause, so I just get whatever cute pictures I can grab. It's as if they simply refuse to acknowledge the existence of most people or the camera most of the time (even if we do a song and dance for their attention). On rare occasions I've been able to grab some really great smiles, but these shots are representative of what they most often do.

July 16, 2006
Wow, just look at Danielle smile for this photo!

The transformation continues. Danielle is more and more engaging. Sophia is now saying simple requests if prompted (i.e. "I want _____.") Danielle actually began dialoguing back-and-forth with us! She is now able to have short (3-4 turn, short sentence) conversations! They both have started to play with toys at this point. They no longer "line things up in a row" all the time. Sophia's hand flapping has greatly reduced and I overheard Danielle actually reply to another child when he greeted her with a hello at church. It is amazing.

First Day of School - August 2005

First Day of School - August 2006

August 2006
Here are just <u>some of the things</u> that the girls do which were "impossible" prior to March 2006…

- Sophia (age 3 ½) will answer and ask "Who's that?" or "What's that?" questions.
- Danielle (age 6) will happily greet me or her dad when we pick her up from school (we used to be met with angry tantrums every single day – for the last 2 years).
- Danielle and I go through each day communicating back and forth about all kinds of little, simple things.
- Danielle will now allow me to get water for her. She sometimes allows me to help her with tasks. (Before she displayed obsessive compulsive behaviors that were so extreme that the most minute task was inexplicably tedious)
- Danielle does not always wipe off touches or kisses anymore.
- The other night I allowed Danielle to fall asleep with me on the couch. It was funny because I had to tell her to "stop talking or go to your own bed." I used to dream of the day I would have to tell her to stop talking.
- They both make really good eye contact now.
- We now have to coax them into the house from playing outside. We used to try all KINDS of tactics to get them to play together or with us outside for more than a

couple of minutes. All they ever wanted to do was watch videos.
- They both now play with toys.
- Danielle responds to the comments, simple questions, and greetings of other <u>children</u>.
- Sophia's torso and legs began to clear up from eczema & dense bumps right away, and now her arms are clearing up as well.
- Their voices are both stronger and more deliberate. They are finding their voices! They are <u>using</u> their voices. Sophia no longer just grunts for everything. What the devil tried to steal, they will use to bring many to the Lord Jesus Christ.

<u>October 2006 Journal Entry</u>
- Some of Sophia's (4 in November) spontaneous phrases:
- "Mommy, I want a drink of wawa."
- "I want _____ (food or movie "voofie")."
- "C'mon, wet's go!"
- She now answers yes and no questions. (Started saying yes about 2 weeks ago.)
- She greets people spontaneously & says goodbye without prompting.
- She sings, claps, raises hands at church. She dances.
- Her first time doing this was in pre-service prayer, in September, singing *Here I Am to Worship* at the top of her lungs. I cried from joy the entire time and could hardly sing myself. Before she would only want us to hold her and she would bury her face during prayer & worship.)
- Danielle does not have as much echolalia (repeat every single word said to her) as she did in September.

- She will now let me pack her lunch & put it in her backpack (a <u>big</u> no-no in September).
- I'm now allowed to help her with her jacket in the morning.
- She now does not mess up her hair and throw a fit after I have just fixed it.
- She spontaneously talks and interacts with other children.
- Her teachers just reported to me that social referencing is now one of her biggest strengths and a tool for learning. This was one of her greatest challenges before!!

<u>December 2006</u>
A year ago I did not even want the morning time to come and I cried every day, determined to find answers from God. Now we are free from OCD (Obsessive Compulsive Disorder – a common symptom of kids diagnosed with Autism) which had tried to get complete control of our household! (Only if you've faced that can you possibly know what I'm talking about.) Danielle used to always say, "Danielle is sad." She has not expressed that for months. Their personalities are coming out and they are enjoying life and people. They are learning to have friends and relate to us. They have also learned to pray and worship God. Not only that, but they've memorized how to preach to others (which they often do if they find an audience) about how to make Jesus your "very best friend." Satan wants to destroy our kids. If he can't kill them, he'll try to kill their voice, personality, and destiny. But we don't have to accept one bit of his plan – because if God is for us, who can be against us? (Romans 8:31)

And then there's little Victoria Alexis (17 months)

She is doing fantastic. Vaccine & pesticide free! She is getting a much less toxic start on life than her sisters did, and she will continue to reap the benefits of a "new and living way" that God has shown to us. She already says words and is very engaging. She loves people, especially her big sisters.

There is an answer for every problem in Jesus Christ. God says in Jeremiah 33:3 , "Call to me and I will answer you." We put this to the test and have found that God does not lie. His presence in our lives is real. That's what Emmanuel means – God <u>*with us*</u>.

Believing with you for miracles,
Pastors Don & Christa Proctor

Luke 15:24
...for this [daughter] of mine was dead and has now returned to life. [She] was lost, but now [she] is found.

CHRISTA PROCTOR

5 What You Don't Know... Can Kill You!

There was a life threatening belief system I had always lived by. It was not one of conscious choice, it was simply always "there" and never up until this point in my life had I ever challenged it. Sure, I would see the occasional article or email spam which consisted of silly little conspiracy theories. And in my mind I scoffed at the poor souls who gave them the time of day. The belief system I'm referring to can pretty much be summed up in this one little statement, "If something were unsafe 'they' wouldn't allow it on the market."

Here's an example. Jennifer was a friend of mine who was always going on and on about the condition of our global food chain. Every time she came over she would bring some strange sounding concoction (flour-less brownies, for instance) as a treat. It was always yummy, but I just didn't get her. I mean, why would a person as busy as she was continually go to all the trouble of making such "strange" foods when you can just easily buy pre-packaged or even pre-made-from-scratch items? One time she felt the need to tell me about the evils of *something* to do with *something* about wheat, and I just sat there wondering what her point was. I kept thinking, if our food was so unsafe, it would not be allowed to be sold in the grocery stores! In my mind I lovingly and humorously thought of her as the "food nazi."

Lo and behold, as a result of our trip to see the detox specialist, I was suddenly thrust into a new realm of special diets and previously unheard of foods. Remember the binder full of protocols for each girl that we were supposed to follow

to the "T"? Within each binder was a list of foods that had to be completely removed from their diets. The list included:
- Gluten grains
- Cow dairy
- Pork
- Canola oil
- Soy
- Peanuts
- MSG
- Black or white pepper
- Cane sugar
- Onions
- No use of microwave oven

At first I was so overwhelmed with keeping track of what herbal & mineral supplements to give them at various times throughout the day, that the food thing was the least of my concerns.

I remember the evening of our visit to the doctor, my mom kept shaking her head thinking that life as I had known it would cease to exist for quite some time.

The cooking. THE COOKING. That was going to be quite a task and she knew it.

We took advantage of being around the doctor and his assistant that week when the girls were getting their daily LED (Laser Energy Detox) treatments. Every day I had a new list of questions about what kinds of oils and seasonings were acceptable. We were given some great tips and I was so happy to discover that Danielle would eat such a thing as Tapioca Bread.

She had become such a picky eater. For instance, she wanted frozen pancakes every morning for breakfast. Not just any brand, either. They absolutely had to be Krusteaz brand or she would not even touch them. I had heard of a GFCF diet (Gluten Free/Casein Free), and determined that I would be reluctantly willing to do it, if and only if the doctor specifically prescribed it for my kids. I just couldn't imagine what Danielle would eat if we had to go on such a diet. Well the GFCF thing was only a small part of what we had to do in changing their dietary intake.

At first I simply followed the "forbidden foods" list without any insight into it. We had invested a huge amount of time and money into this thing, and what good would it do if we were not committed to following through with *whatever* we'd been instructed? Whether or not it made sense to us, we interviewed enough doctors and families to trust in our decision to be there in the first place. I guess you could call it blind faith, but on the other hand there were proven results from other families who had walked the road ahead of us. The few families who had success represented the rewards of faith and diligence. I learned enough to know that their success was directly related to the degree with which they carried out the specific instructions for their child's unique biomedical needs.

Remembering the lady who had spent all that time with me on the phone, I quickly ran and bought the book she had told me about. It is called <u>Nourishing Traditions</u>, by Sally Fallon. Every night, once the kids went to bed, I would read it word by word, highlighting every sentence I didn't fully grasp. There may have been more words highlighted than not. I read every book about food I could get my hands on, as long as it was not sponsored by any type of major food producer or the

USDA. All of a sudden the "food nazi's" words began to resonate inside the corners of my mind. She wasn't radical after all! She was onto something. I couldn't wait to talk with her and pick her brain about food. I thought, *"She must be full of other vital information I could use right now!"*

Every week at the grocery store I painstakingly read the ingredients label of each item before purchasing it, not knowing what most of the ingredients were on many labels. The first time doing this it took me 3 hours to get through the store. It quickly hit me that not just any grocery store would do. In the places I normally shopped, I could now only buy foods from possibly 2-3 aisles in the entire store. I was in shock. And when I peered into the carts of other shoppers I felt like Neo in the movie, "The Matrix." I had taken the "red pill" and was now awake for the first time. I saw everyone around me in the grocery store as being trapped in this matrix of deception, unwittingly spending hard earned money on synthetic food, filled with all kinds of chemicals and wreaking havoc in the bodies and minds of precious family members.

The more I read about food, the more I got a revelation about that "forbidden foods list" given to us by the doctor. It was all starting to make sense. Almost all of the foods on that list were things that *no* human body was designed to process. At least not in the food's readily available form. What was puzzling to me at first is that so many of the items are marketed as "health" products. Again, why would that be allowed if these things are so unsafe? Here's another startling discovery: MSG has over 200 names, such as "natural flavorings" and "natural seasonings." You really have to be careful.

As you can imagine, even in a health food or specialty market, it's nearly impossible to find ready-made foods which do not contain canola oil or soy. I learned to cook everything from scratch that we fed to our kids. And because there were two of them, my husband and I decided it would be best and simplest for us to adopt their diet as well. This decision made even more sense when I learned about the difference between real food & synthetic food, fast food and slow food.

People often asked me, "What *do* you eat?" Well, I was pleasantly surprised to discover the answer to this myself. The fact is that you can still eat pretty much everything you already enjoy eating. You simply eat the "real" or "authentic" version of it. Let's take Spaghetti as an example. It's probably safe to say that many people make spaghetti by boiling noodles, browning some meat with onions & seasonings, and pouring in a jar of sauce. I now simply ensure that all of my ingredients are as free from toxins or glutens as possible. So here's what I do. I use either grass fed organic ground beef, or I use ground bison which is generally minimally processed anyway. My kids had an intolerance to onions, but shallots were ok for them. So I brown the meat with shallots, sea salt, organic italian herbs, and fresh organic garlic. In a different pan I sauté (in extra virgin organic coconut oil) some shallots, celery, carrots, garlic, whatever other veggies I want. Once those are tender, I add a large can of organic tomatoes, sea salt, basil, balsamic vinegar, and let that simmer for 20-30 minutes. I run that through the food processor because my kids don't like the chunks. Instead of regular pasta I buy organic brown rice noodles. It's super easy, doesn't take too long, and we love it!

The fact of the matter is there are more neurotransmitters connected to your "gut" (your intestinal tract, which runs from your mouth to your anus) than the amount that exist in your brain. What you eat has a direct affect upon you neurologically. When you realize that you ARE what you eat, the word "diet" will have new meaning for you. Don't even think in terms of weight loss. In fact, most obesity in the US is a result of our bodies being unable to process the foods we eat. It's not as much a matter of *how much* we eat, as much as it is *what* we eat. What if obesity was more of an "allergic reaction" of our bodies to these synthetic substances contained in our food? Or an intolerance our bodies have to the byproducts that occur during the manufacturing and processing of our food and beverages? What about other diseases and disorders?

And it's not just what we put *into* our bodies. What about all the things we put *on* our bodies? Prior to spending thousands of dollars and painstaking follow-up effort to pull an array of certain harmful chemicals out of our girls' bodies. I became keenly aware of what chemicals we allowed them to bath in, etc. Your skin is your largest organ, your body's first line of defense, and also a very high tech mechanism for transporting substances in and out of your body. This book is not intended to fully educate anyone about such things. I am in no way an expert on anything other than the telling of our own experience. These principles are simply part of our own discovery and played a part in building our personal philosophy of how to maintain a safe household environment for our family.

So, how did we make it all work? Here are several steps that I took and also some principles that we began to incorporate into running our household.

1. We did a lot of research to find physicians who were on the cutting edge of recovery protocols. We were willing to sell our home or cars if necessary in order to find the money for our girls to be seen by a holistic practitioner with a proven track record. Armed with a unique protocol for each girl's specific biological needs, we committed to moving heaven and earth in order to stick with the program.

2. I took an entire day and emptied our pantry of every food item that contained our "forbidden ingredients." I actually put them in grocery bags and gave them to neighbors. Part of me felt guilty for passing the "poison" on to them, but my mission was not to convert anyone to our new-found way of living.

3. I loaded up all toxic cleaners and detergents (Formula 409, Tilex and the like had been part of our family's cleaning regime for generations). This is where the pocket book really began to feel the heat because I felt like I was throwing money away. Amazingly, I soon discovered a very effective non-toxic line of cleaners sold in concentrated form from Shaklee. I bought a bottle which has lasted me over 3 years. I'm still using that same bottle. And it's a great cleaner! So I've actually saved a lot of money on cleaning products.

4. We got rid of the cordless phones and wireless internet in our home. We stopped using our microwave completely (Before this I used mine constantly). We limited cell phone usage and to this day will not use a Bluetooth ear piece. Electromagnetic waves are definitely hazardous to our health. These findings have become a major concern with many doctors and scientists. Can you imagine the

implications of initiating any type of a "pulling back" in this area of technology? Not only has it become an almost essential part of every day modern life, but the industry itself would try and squash any widespread news of such dangers. It's a big mountain to tackle to say the least. We only took on creating a safety zone in our tiny part of the world. That's something anyone can do and still have a good impact on your health.

5. I asked to be notified by the school district whenever they were going to spray pesticides on the school grounds. There is a vast amount of data about the harm this can do.

6. We made sure there were meal ingredients in our pantry and refrigerator at all times. If there is food in the house, it will be eaten. And it's much better to spend 30 minutes preparing a delicious meal than it is to take 30 minutes and run out for fast food or restaurant food. You have more time at home, there are often leftovers, and it simply tastes better. If your pantry or fridge contain nothing with which you can build a meal, that's when you're in trouble.

7. We decide when and what the kids eat. They decide how much. This is actually a great piece of advice that I got from our first pediatrician. It's so true that kids will NOT starve themselves to death. My kids went several meals without eating because they didn't want to try something outside of their extremely limited meal choice, especially in the beginning. But you cannot imagine what they learned to crave. Hey, this was not without meltdowns or tantrums, but we pressed on - enduring the immediate "pain" - for the ultimate prize and joy that was set firmly

in our hearts. You have to be more determined than the tantrum.

8. We were in regular communication with all their teachers, specialists, and therapists regarding their new diet. Everyone was very supportive. The teachers always made me aware of any class parties so that I could provide alternatives for my girls to enjoy. Many times the entire class would partake of what we brought.

9. This was a team effort. There is no doubt that I did most of the research, the cooking, and setting up the home. But my husband was a team player in every sense of the word. He was always open to listening to some new interesting piece of the food or medical or behavioral puzzle. He flexed his work schedule a little bit so that he could help administer all of the morning supplements and feed them breakfast in the mornings before school. He never complained, but took ownership of the process any way he possibly could.

10. We simplified life wherever possible. Other than regularly volunteering to serve our community through our local church and the occasional school volunteer assignment, we had to cut back on every activity outside the home. For about a year we limited our social engagements, keeping a weekly date night sacred, and generally tried to be home as much as possible. Maintaining a routine was an enormous factor toward the success of following through with the medical protocol.

11. We mixed everything we did with faith. Every meal prepared, every supplement administered, every therapy session embarked upon, BELIEVING that it was making a

difference for the good! If you're just doing something to go through the motions, or worse...doing it with fear and worry in your heart, I'm telling you it's not going to have the desired effect. Whatever you do, mix it with faith. Energy is energy. Just like a microwave oven can send unseen negative energy through the atmosphere, so can fear and worry and doubt! Believe in what you're doing. Believe it's making a difference.

6 Working the Inside-Out and the Outside-In

The Body-Soul-Spirit UNION

It's more than "getting the metal out."
It's more than a special diet.
It's more than behavioral therapy.
It's doing *everything* and all at once.

The role that digestive health plays in contributing to mental/emotional/physical/neurological health cannot be overemphasized. And let me tell you that you won't hear anything taught in mainstream education or spoken over the television airwaves that contradicts the food industry's bought-and-paid-for nutritional doctrine. After all, most news programs are financially sponsored by big food & drug companies. At the risk of sounding like a conspiracy theorist, I hope you will take my advice and open your mind to the possibility that what you were taught in school, what the nutritionists are taught, what is reported in food-and-drug-company-sponsored news programs or cooking shows, may just be simply inaccurate yet financially expedient.

With that said, let's delve into our body ecology a little bit deeper.

Body Ecology. Is this something you've ever even thought about? I never did unless it was to cram for a biology test in high school. I actually never liked science when I was growing up, and I now find it to be very important in my every day life. *Why, oh why, didn't I pay more attention back in school science classes?*

Let me share with you a few of the ways in which your body ecology can be affected for the good or the bad, and how it directly affects your physical well being, your mood, your mental faculties, basically everything about you. Think of your body as the most technologically advanced union of electricity, chemicals, organic tissue, and life-force (or your spirit/your mind).

If you find it a strange or novel concept that your spirit, personality or mood would be immediately and directly affected by physical inputs, then consider this scenario. The other day I was at work and was sorting through some items that needed to be put away in the back room. Among the items was a small but heavy piece of metal. I was crouched down to pick it up and as I began to stand, the metal item slipped out of my hand. It fell about 3-4 feet down and landed directly on my big toe. There was an immediate and direct affect on my entire mood. It was a real "downer" and also made me angry at the same time. I actually was also stunned and could not really utter a sound for a few seconds. Even my ability to listen to anything that was being said to me was greatly hindered. I knew my co-workers were speaking but was unable to process what they were saying at the moment. That single hit to my physical body affected my mind, my mood, personality, everything. My spirit really had to make the choice to rally all my faculties together and make it a great day.

So what if we take the same analogy but instead of a single episode of harm being inflicted upon an external member of our body, we look at the example of an internal part (or multiple parts) of our body being continually assaulted? Take it down to the cellular level. Isn't it true that an assault upon our bodies at the cellular level would potentially have the same type of effects as those I experienced when the metal item hit my big toe? I would venture to say, even more so. It may be more difficult to detect and the effect may not appear to be as immediate, but over time the results/symptoms might be the same if not worse than what I momentarily experienced.

So what, you may ask, does this have to do with Autism? Everyone is so concerned about our earth's ecology (and rightly so). If we keep a good balance in nature then the things of the earth can thrive and the earth can continue to provide good things for us as humans. And a crucial factor in our personal ability to thrive is the ecology of our own human bodies.

In my opinion, Autism is a condition in which many factors come together. Here's my somewhat self-educated theory in a nutshell. Every family line has distinct genetic vulnerabilities, each blood type has vulnerabilities, the male and female sex each have their own vulnerabilities, etc. Environmental exposures will exploit each genetic vulnerability. Environmental triggers would include the following: things that are in our food, things that are in the air, things passed from the mother in the womb, EMFs (electromagnetic frequencies), words that are spoken, thoughts and intentions, the way in which we do immunizations, etc. These factors all come together to create "the perfect storm." What manifests as Autism in one individual may very well manifest as Diabetes, Crohn's, Asthma, or Cancer in another individual. We must stop treating symptoms and start addressing root issues. If we would be more discriminating about what we put in and on

our bodies, as well as what we speak and listen to, we would see diseases be reversed and healed on a more regular basis.
This is what I mean by the term "Deception of Disease." If you think about it, diseases don't really exist in the way many of us think they do. For instance, I had thought that Autism was a disease which causes neurological problems and developmental delays, etc. Or I used to think that Diabetes was a disease which caused a whole set of its own symptoms. You get the idea...basically I thought that different diseases cause different sets of symptoms to occur.

But here's the truth of the matter. Each disease is simply a label for a set of symptoms. That label is just a name, and not a name for any root problem, mind you. Think of it as a category. A way to sort symptoms into groups. Once we understand this, the disease begins to unravel in our minds. Instead of taking on a big scary disease, we start to think of the disease as a name, a mere byproduct of root causes. Many of which are simple to address at the source. However, our culture is indoctrinated in such a way that we often only treat the symptoms. We are convinced that the symptoms are the roots. They are not, they are "the fruit" and the diagnoses or disease is merely a name which groups together sets of symptoms.

Often we take medications which merely mask the symptoms but simultaneously present a new set of inherent risks. Not to worry, there are more medications to treat the side-effects of the original meds. And so goes the cycle of "cover-up". Instead of addressing the cause, we simply cover it up. If we treated infected wounds in this way they would never heal, but only get worse, spreading throughout our system and causing great damage. This damage would not only infiltrate the rest of our physical body tissue, but also our emotions. Our very personality would be affected because of the illness from that infection. So, what's the difference between the external/seen vs. internal/unseen cause & effect? Nothing.

All this to say, you simply cannot isolate the condition of your physical body from the condition of your soul, your personality, your emotions, your spirit. The condition of one facet of your being will manifest in the other facets of your being. Because of this, you must allow the remedies to be worked from the outside in, and from the inside out. All at once. From the physical to the emotional to the spiritual parts of what makes up YOU.

I used to see the body, the soul (mind/will/emotions), and the spirit (life-force) of a person as three connected, related, but somewhat separate parts. Not that anyone ever really taught that to me. But in my understanding it was like this, "I am a spirit, I have a soul, and I live in a body." That thought is still true in my mind but to me it falls short of really conveying an accurate image of the relationship of our 3 parts. Much more than a connection between the three, there exists an actual UNION *of* the three. Indiscernible as to exactly how and where the interconnect of the three parts occur.

Imagine the SOUL as the actual switcher between the spirit and the body. Any input from the physical realm will affect the soul, which will in turn affect the spirit. This can be for the good or for the bad. Likewise, any input generated by your spirit will be processed through your soul (mind/will/emotions) and be transferred into the physical realm of your body. In this way the 3 parts can work in harmony and unity with one another...to your health, or to your detriment.

Remember how in chapter 3 of this book, I said that we decided to approach our girls' health from every angle? We wanted to leave no stone unturned. Well, you cannot address things in the physical realm without affecting things in the spiritual realm. The very atmosphere of your home and your life will be affected. The opposite is also true. If you address things in the unseen realms, the realm of the spirit, there will be an impact upon the physical well-being of your family.

7 So How is This Done?

The first step in gaining understanding about health is to start with a blank canvas. I'm not saying to forget everything you've ever learned, but be willing to put it on the table and make all things negotiable that are not explicit in Scripture. If you've stuck with the book this far, you're obviously in it because you're desperate for some new insight. Well it's impossible to gain new insight if we are not teachable. Hold what you think you already know with an open hand. Be willing for your opinions to change. I promise, if you're stubborn about knowledge then you're stuck, so go no further.

Since I'm not a doctor or nutritionist, I make no claims or pretense in being able to advise you specifically on what you should or should not do for treating your body. However, I do recommend taking the following steps if you plan to go to war against Autism or any other disease and its effects on your loved one.

In the Physical Realm:

1 Consult with a reputable physician who has experienced measurable success in helping recover others (not simply in treating symptoms) from the disease or disorder that is facing you. Make lots of phone calls. I personally contacted 15 physicians before making our final selection. And once I made the selection I spoke with 2 families that had already been treated by that particular physician before we kept our appointment. The caliber of physician we're talking about may likely have a waiting list of several months. It's worth it. And in the meantime, ask if there are books or articles with information he/she would recommend.

2. Be ready to make a financial investment and sacrifice. The doctor visits and treatments will probably be very expensive and not covered by insurance. I have found that most people find a way to afford family toys, cars, coffee, clothes, etc. Where there is a will, there is a way. Pray and ask God for help. He has come through for us every time. At the right time. My husband likes to say, "He's seldom early but never late."

3. Follow their advice to the letter for at least 12 months. Certain afflicting food proteins and particles, as well as parasites or toxins, may take a minimum of 6-9 months before they are completely eradicated from the body and you begin to see real changes. With the time and money we invested, we determined to be very legalistic about the protocol, wanting to give it every chance to work. We are very glad we did.

4. READ. There are so many wonderful books to help guide you. Even if you decided not to see a doctor, you can benefit so much from the books and blogs that I recommend.

5. Eat unprocessed, simple food. The fewer ingredients, the better, if you are buying something that has ingredients. If you cannot pronounce one of the ingredients then I would say stay away from it. You'll be amazed how easy it is to cook great tasting food. I stuck with the basics in the beginning. Roasted whole chicken with sea salt and fresh garlic & herbs, placing organic veggies in the roasting pan. Mmmmm, my whole family loves it. Can't get easier than that!

OK, so you get the idea. Be open to change. Be strong and stick with your regimen for at least 12 months. That goes by with the blink of an eye!

In the Invisible Realm

Wherever you are at in life, if you're not yet able to see that there is an invisible realm which is as real and as accessible as anything you can physically sense, then I urge you to be open to all that I have left to say. It's not my goal to convince or convert you, because such things only come by revelation when one is ready to see and hear.

Without a doubt, the progress our girls have experienced in coming out of the tentacles of Autism Spectrum Disorder, have been in large part due to the war that has been waged in the dimension of the soul and the spirit. This is not as mysterious as it may sound. You may even be surprised to learn how simple it is. I believe this may be why so many people don't take advantage of these "weapons" if you will. I speak in these terms because I see disease and disorder as an enemy which seeks to entrap and enslave us with symptoms and behaviors that inhibit our ability to be who we really are, say what we want to say, and do what we desire to do.

One of the symptoms our oldest daughter is facing right now is that she expresses the exact opposite of what she truly desires. For example she wants more than anything to see a certain friend at a social gathering and to say hello to that friend. Yet an obsession tries to overtake her in which she incessantly talks of nothing more and says that she is NOT going to see that friend. If I tell her, "OK you don't need to see _____," she begins to cry and say that she WILL say hello. Yet when the friend is found she may say angry words and/or be unwilling to say hello at all...until the friend is out of sight and then more crying. I am telling you, this is no way for a person to live -- in a prison of compulsion that drives one to disagree with their own desires. This is what steals a person's dreams and destiny right out from under them if it is allowed to stay.

This is where I get militant. Not against people or their opinions, but against any evil that would hold my children, their dreams or abilities captive. About this we cannot afford to be passive. When I get angry it's taken out on forces of darkness that are affected by or are affecting the physical realm.

For every physical condition there is a corresponding spirit. You know this. Walk into an ICU, and the atmosphere is completely different than the healthy new-born room of the hospital. Call it energy or atmosphere...you're talking about the unseen world. The realm of the spirit. You can feel it yourself - a spirit of joy, a spirit of peace, a spirit of love, of faith. On the other hand, there are spirits of discouragement, depression, disappointment, defeat, and so on. If you have been physically wounded or compromised then a vulnerability to dark spiritual oppression exists. Any time you've been bullied, abused, or talked down to, spirits of darkness attach themselves to those unseen wounds and want to stay there. Their influence can affect our emotional and physical well-being. Their influence can over a period of time generate symptoms which medications have been created to treat. As you can see, if we pursue health in the physical sense only, our progress will be limited and we will get to a certain point and become stuck.

It's a Process - Going from Breakthrough to Breakthrough:
As with the avenues and pathways to address healing in the natural (food, natural remedies, etc.), this spiritual roadmap to health will at first appear confusing and overwhelming. Don't think of where you are now, where you want to go, and all possible points in between. Simply keep the goal in your heart and don't let go of it. Start where you are and ask God to customize your spiritual path in the same way that your physical path is unique to your own make-up.

He alone knows the specific time and place of the inner, unseen wounds that exist. He will guide us in unraveling all mysteries - one step after another. Don't worry about all that needs to be addressed. Simply ask Him to bring issues to the surface as needed and show you what to do with them. It's a spiritual detoxification process. It's also a spiritual war, so be strong and courageous!

With each spiritual breakthrough, you will see a corresponding advancement in the physical realm. Sometimes the physical symptoms even seem to spike and grow worse after a spiritual victory. I like to consider this the "last ditch effort" of the darkness to hang on. The darkness does not like to be expelled and will try and intimidate you and get you to let go of your confidence and faith. The darkness tries to intimidate you by creating an illusion that things are actually getting worse, so that you will lose heart and simply give up the fight. **But what do you have to lose by believing? Nothing.** So just keep believing and stand firm in your confidence that the darkness *will* go.

We must also withstand the temptation to settle for gains that fall short of our original vision or goal. My vision for our children is that they will be completely symptom free from any symptoms of Autism. They have already made so much progress that most people who meet them would never guess that they were diagnosed. We can now dialog with them about many things, and they are able to make friends to a certain degree. It would be very tempting to say, "This is as good as it gets." But I stir up the warrior spirit inside of me from time to time. My girls will thank me for this one day when they are able to have friendships with all kinds of people and discuss things to whatever level they wish. There will come a day when their choices are not dictated by ability, but only by personal desires.

Understanding the Power of your Opinions:

In our experience, probably the most important "weapon" we've learned to use in this war is that of love and acceptance of others. Doesn't that seem ironic? Love is the greatest weapon we could ever use against the powers of darkness. The more we learned how to love and accept others, the more healing our kids have experienced.

We live in a very judgmental society. Everyone has an opinion about others and they usually don't keep those opinions to themselves. We used to fall into this trap and during our process, God showed us that we were very judgmental. The problem with judging others is that the very same attitude of judgment that you dole out is what comes back on you (and on your descendants).

Judging others in this fashion equates to a poverty of the soul. When we judge other people it's because we have a poverty mentality. A poverty mentality is one of stinginess and withholding. Poverty will not give because it's afraid of not having. When we judge someone we withhold giving them the benefit of the doubt. We withhold giving them grace and understanding. But a generous soul will be made rich! And the problem with having an impoverished soul is that you suffer in the physical realm because of it. You will prosper and be in health in direct correspondence to the degree to which your soul is prosperous. If you have an impoverished soul, you will have an impoverished life. You can be rich with money yet have an impoverished life. Prosperity is more than having money.

When you release people from judgment it means you give up your right to have an opinion about the behavior and actions of others. Do you honestly know why people do the things they do and are the way they are? Think it through before you answer. You think you know, but you honestly don't know what is in the hearts and minds of others. Judging others is when you observe their behavior or actions and presume to know *why* they are doing what they're doing.

It's ok to observe, take note, and determine for yourself - based on their behavior - what degree of relationship you would have with them on a personal level. But to go beyond that and presume to know the reasons for the things you see in their life, well that is to judge them. If you will open yourself up to change in this area, you will be amazed to discover the frequency with which you judge other people. I know I was.

It's very simple. Ask God to show you each time you have made a judgment that has come back on you or your family and is now holding you captive. Live your life and don't worry about trying to think of these judgments on your own. At the right time, God will bring it to the forefront of your mind...a judgment you've made. And then it's your responsibility to say aloud, "God, forgive me for judging _____ for _____. I renounce that judgment and release them right now." You will be amazed at the corresponding progress that will manifest in the physical realm, because the darkness that was attached to that judgment now has no footing and must depart from the situation.

One of the many times God revealed such a thing to me was not long after I'd asked Him to simply bring up any judgments I'd made. I was driving down the road (I can still remember the exact location) not even thinking about it, when suddenly to the forefront of my mind came a statement I had made as a child. I said it as a general statement but in my heart I meant it toward my sister. My exact words were, "I cannot tolerate slowness." My sister is highly intelligent but we have very different personalities and learning styles. In my pride I felt like my way of thinking was always the best, and in my mind, I placed a judgment on the way she processed information. Anyway, 20+ years later, there I was driving down the road, and that judgment was brought to the surface of my soul. Immediately I vocally renounced it and prayed the simple prayer of repentance I stated in the previous paragraph. Within a week our 3-year-old Sophia began answering "yes/no" questions for the first time in her life. This was not a step, but a leap forward for her, and I know it was related. There have been many such related instances.

Why ask "Why?"
Another sign of an impoverished soul is when we continue to ask, "Why me?" or "Why my child?" Listen, you cannot believe in good without believing in evil. And the very simple answer to that question is found in I Peter 5:7-9 "Be sober, be vigilant; because your adversary the devil walks about like a roaring lion, seeking whom he may devour. Resist him, steadfast in the faith, knowing that the same sufferings are experienced by your brotherhood in the world."

Since before time began, the Devil has been at war with the Creator Father God. Yes, I'm saying it...Satan. Satan hates God and it's the one true story from which every other story is derived. Satan is out for blood and his only purpose toward the sons and daughters of the Father is to kill, steal from, and destroy humanity. That's all he offers: death and destruction. God on the other hand, only offers life and freedom and every good and perfect gift. There is no light in Satan. And there is no darkness in God, who paid for all the sins of man with the blood of His very own Son, Jesus, so that everyone who believes upon Jesus will not pay for their own sin but will have everlasting life.

The very earth itself groans and yearns for humanity to understand all of this and take our rightful place in the fullness of what has been purchased for us through the death and resurrection of Jesus. So, you see, it's a battle that began before time and only through accepting the Victor do we position ourselves as overcomers. Because in and of ourselves, it's impossible to be saved from the fallenness of creation. But through Christ, we have been made *more* than conquerors.

So the "Why Me?" answer is clear. The Devil is the enemy and wants to ravage God's children and creation. Whether or not we believe this, it's the truth. In my life I've won and lost, but in the end I do understand who gets the blame for the bad. Devil=bad, God=good. Period. If I sit around asking "Why me?" then I am working against the very faith that will move the victory closer to me. That's a waste of time and a distraction to sap my energy. Satan even goes so far as to use religious statements like, "God must be trying to teach you something through this." But Jesus made it clear...He said, "If you've seen me, you've seen the Father." Not once did Jesus put sickness or calamity on an individual. He came for one purpose: "that we might have life, and that more abundant." All we need to know is that if it's destructive it's not from God. And if God is for us, what can possibly withstand us?

Why in the world would I believe for my girls to be well or even go to extreme lengths to pursue their health if I believed it was their destiny to have Autism? Or that God somehow meant for them to have it. Wouldn't I be fighting against the will of God (or if you don't believe in God -- "the cosmos") in doing so?

Guard Your Words and Thoughts
Nothing can set the course of your life or affect the atmosphere around you like your words and thoughts. Time and time again we are taught in Scripture about the importance and power of our words and thoughts.

Proverbs 18:20 "Death and life are in the power of the tongue: and they that love it shall eat the fruit thereof."

Philippians 4:8 "Finally, brethren, whatsoever things are true, whatsoever things are honest, whatsoever things are just, whatsoever things are pure, whatsoever things are lovely, whatsoever things are of good report; if there be any virtue, and if there be any praise, think on these things."

We could go on and on about this, and many books have been written on the subject of what the Bible says regarding our words and thoughts. But here I would like to explain to you that your words are containers of energy - literally, they emit measurable frequencies into the atmosphere. When thoughts of doubt enter your mind from the enemy of your soul, speak aloud words of hope. Declare with your voice and write down on paper a description of what you are believing for.

Sometimes I have literally shouted out words of hope so that the discouragement around me would be silenced. Sometimes I sing out the words. Other times I write them out. The words of God are the most powerful words we can utter. I have written out long passages of Scripture which I desire to see manifest in the lives of my children. I place their names within the Scripture in my notebook, and then I pray to God using these very scriptures with their names. I not only make requests to God, but I also make proclamations and commandments, using His authority and His very word. Here are 2 examples from my journal. There are many more.

Psalm 57
In the shadow of Your wings I will take refuge TILL THE STORMS OF DESTRUCTION PASS BY." The Proctors cry out to God MOST HIGH, to God who fulfills His purpose for us. He will send from heaven and SAVE us; He will put to shame [anyone or anything] who tramples on us. ...They [the spirits of darkness] set a net for our steps; our souls WERE bowed down. They dug a pit in my way, but

> *THEY have fallen into it themselves! My heart is STEADFAST. (My answer:) I will SING and MAKE MELODY! Awake! My glory! (my whole being) The Proctors will give thanks to You, oh Lord, among the peoples. WE WILL sing your praises to you among the NATIONS.*
>
> *Psalm 58:10-11*
> *The Proctors will rejoice when they see the vengeance (upon Autism); we will bathe our feet in the blood of [diseases]! Mankind will say, "Surely there is a reward for the righteous; surely there is a God who judges on the earth." AMEN!*

Time and time again I would think upon these Scriptures, pray them aloud, as well as many others like them. I use ANY encouraging words or phrases that come along. There are two iron words that hang above my stovetop so that I would be reminded in the place where I was spending so much of my time. The two words are simply, "Relax. Believe." The background noise of our home was usually kids' movies which reminded me to "just keep swimming," "keep moving forward," and "The sun will come out tomorrow." My favorite commercial was from Kleenex which said, "My tears don't compromise my strength." I rephrased that and would tell myself, "My tears don't compromise my faith."

Yes, there were many days filled with tears and frustration, but that's why we need faith. If everything looked ok or felt ok, then we wouldn't need to believe in what we can't see...hoping against hope! Some would call it foolishness, but I'm telling you what I know to be true. There is no reason to stop believing. I don't care what the odds are, the diagnosis, the facts. What do you have to lose by believing?

Christa Proctor

8   Where Are They Now?

It's completely astonishing at how fast time has flown from the time we first wondered about Danielle's development, before Sophia was even born. For years it was an mountainous climb such that the summit was not even in view. But since about 2009 we began the downward descent and started to feel like we had overcome. I'd say that we're still walking steadily down the mountain, but that life has become brighter with each passing day, week, month, and year.

It wasn't even a year ago (Danielle was 9, Sophia, 7, and Victoria 4) that the girls began regularly role playing with their dolls. The lack of this skill had greatly hindered their ability to connect with typically developing kids, but they eventually got it! The fact that it came later in life isn't in and of itself a bad thing. They have retained a sense of innocence that I don't see in most typical 8 & 10 year olds. That's a blessing.

Danielle is attending our neighborhood elementary school for the first time ever. Having moved here before the school even broke ground, we'd never been able to send her there because of the necessity of specialized education. She is in a mainstream class for most of the day and is pulled out for certain subjects. I'll be honest, she's fallen behind academically, but socially it has been a stellar year for her. She's in fourth grade and shares genuine, honest-to-goodness mutual friendship with typically developing girls of her own age. This has never happened before! Already this year she's had four birthday party invitations, and they were not the type of party where the entire class was invited. You see, until now I cannot remember Danielle being invited to an intimate birthday party of any typically developing peer. She's been included in family "everyone-come" type parties, or to parties of much younger children, which she also loves. But this is different. It's been the same group of girls at each party.

I was so concerned about her social success before this school-year began, but we trusted God. At this year's IEP I could tell that the educators and administrators were nervous when they had to explain to me that they were concerned about the school's ability to keep her on track academically. They just don't have a special day class set up for that. But I had opted out of the district's special day class because it was on a different campus, and I just knew in my gut that she needed the amazing atmosphere of her current school. During that IEP I explained to the team that for our family, this year was all about Danielle's social and relational success. They reported no behavioral problems whatsoever, which is another first at school!

Sophia is still in a wonderful special day class, which we love. It's a three-year program and as a second grader she can attend the class one more year. One or both of the girls have had this special teacher for three years now, so she knows our kids pretty well. She's the best at what she does, and again, that what we've always prayed for our kids -- to have the best.

Sophia has surprised us all with her academic pursuit. She's not above average in that regard, but she doesn't resist the work. She grasps math and English concepts fairly well considering the comprehension challenges she still has to overcome in verbal conversation.

She loves music and has gone from being the child who would bury her head in our chests and look no one in the eye, to being the child who wants to sing a solo at Christmas. And she's great at it! This year at Christmas she sang a duet with another little girl. The song was so fitting and the girls did an amazing job. Needless to say, there was not a dry eye in the house. The song is "When You Believe" from The Prince of Egypt. Here are some of the lyrics that Sophia sang:

> ...Now we are not afraid, although we know there's much to fear.
>
> We were climbing mountains long before we knew we could.
>
> ...Yet now I'm standing here, my heart so full I can't explain.
>
> Seeking faith and speaking words I never thought I would.
>
> (The chorus has become a new anthem for me:)
>
> There can be miracles when you believe. Though hope is frail, it's hard to kill.
>
> Who knows what miracles you can achieve. When you believe somehow you will.
>
> You will when you believe.

We put the girls in softball last spring. Unfortunately the first 7 years (for Sophia) and 9 years (Danielle) of their lives were so busy with hours and hours of therapy each week, this was their first experience in a community sport. By this age most of the players were already pretty good. It's a recreational league, but some of the families were pretty serious about winning and playing well. However, we had nothing but positive experiences with each of the players, coaches, and parents. Sophia wants to play again this year. But Danielle wants to sign up for ballet.

We still have much ground to take. More land to clear. More giants to kill. But God has done so much for us, and we have weathered so many dark storms that we truly are not afraid. We still employ the same tactics described in this book on a daily basis regarding our words, thoughts, and seeking God for wisdom.

By the beginning of 2008 I had grown physically weary because of strictly following all of the protocols, combined with hours of therapies, training, and having two more precious babies (and a miscarriage at 16 weeks in between the birth of these two). Every January we embark on a 21-day season of special prayer and fasting. It's a time to get clarity from God about the year. That year a sense of release came to me regarding the strictness of the diet and supplements. It was time for a break. We didn't go back to our old ways of eating, but we did ease up a little bit. We instituted an 80%-20% principle. For instance we started having pizza, popcorn and root beer on Friday nights. I advocate following the leading of God in all these things. We didn't decide to do this because it was the easy thing to do, but because we felt a release from God. He told me, "You've done well. Now let Me finish up some of these areas before moving on."

It's now January 2011 and we're in the middle of our annual prayer and fasting. We're asking God for wisdom, feeling a new press coming on. Our strength is being renewed for the fight, and we are ready to advance once again. One of the things for which God has made a way is HBOT, Hyperbaric Oxygen Therapy. Interestingly enough, the people who originally pointed us to the truth about Autism are the ones who we've gone back to just one month ago for the HBOT. I'm speaking of the doctor and her husband, who referred us to the generationrescue.org site and also to the specialist who set the detox protocols for our girls.

At the end of this book I've included the blog posts which chronicle the first three HBOT sessions and results. You can find more updates at deceptionofdisease.com.

The journey continues, but I know what happens in the end. We win.

My friends, I have no cookie-cutter answers to offer. If one family is encouraged, strengthened, or even dares to pursue complete recovery for their loved one, then it's worth every minute of time it took me to write this little book. More than anything, I want you to understand that healing and recovery are POSSIBLE. People may try and say that our daughters must not have been very affected in the first place. I am the last person on earth that wanted to accept the harsh reality with which we were faced. I can say this with confidence. We once were lost in this tangled puzzle of autism, but now we are found. I once was blind to many things, but now I can see. My children were for all intents and purposes, unable to truly hear or speak, and now they can.

The most valuable knowledge I could possibly share with you is that God is on your side. He did not PLACE you in a difficult path. There is a popular religious thought which is very untrue. It goes something like this, "God won't give you any more than you can bear." There are several problems with this statement. The first being it's often quoted as if it's from the Bible when it actually is not at all. Here is what the Scripture actually says, and it has nothing at all to do with problems being given to you by God.

I Corinthians 10:12-13 Therefore let anyone who thinks that he stands take heed lest he fall. No temptation has overtaken you that is not common to man. God is faithful, and he will not let you be tempted beyond your ability, but with the temptation he will also provide the way of escape, that you may be able to endure it.

Paul is writing to people in Chapter 10 and warning them not to desire evil. He was specifically telling them to be careful not to willfully enter into a situation where they know they will be tempted to do evil. His point was that if you do find yourself in a temptation, remember that God will provide you a way of escape so that you can withstand the temptation to do evil. The source of temptation is made clear in the book of James

James 1:12-14 Blessed is the one who perseveres under trial because, having stood the test, that person will receive the crown of life that the Lord has promised to those who love him. When tempted, no one should say, "God is tempting me." For God cannot be tempted by evil, nor does he tempt anyone; but each person is tempted when they are dragged away by their own evil desire and enticed.

Disease and trouble are not God's will for anyone. Difficulties come and are a part of life. He's the one who is our Helper, Healer, Redeemer, Savior. Whatever cards you or your child has been dealt, if we give them to God, He will make a winning hand out of them every time. What the enemy means for our harm, God will cause to have a meaning for good. The enemy is more patient than we are and will not give up as easily as we humans often do. If he can use religious sayings to put the blame on God for the evil he has caused, then his work is easy. If we think God is the source or author of the problem, then how will we run to Him with confidence for the answers?

You can trust God. He is the One person that will not disappoint you. Simply ask Him to prove Himself to you. Don't take my word for it. If what I'm saying is true - if He really is your loving Father Creator, and Jesus Christ is His Son - then He can convince you of that Himself. If you aren't sure but want to be sure, just ask Him to reveal Himself to you. If it's a lie then nothing will happen and you've lost nothing. But if Jesus really is the Son of God and the One who is the Way, the Truth, and the Life that will bring every answer you need, then He's able to speak to you in a way that you will know it.

What is your dream? What is it worth? If it meant that you had to fight the good fight of faith and keep believing for 2 years before seeing the fulfillment, is it worth it? What about 10 years? Would it be worth it to you if you had to press on and believe for 25, 30, 50 years? We decided long ago, that if it meant we spend our lifetime reaching and believing for this...it will have been worth it. And I believe my kids will agree.

CHRISTA PROCTOR

{ SUPPLEMENTAL }

POSTS FROM THE BLOG
deceptionofdisease.com

POST #1

OUR FIRST HYPERBARIC OXYGEN EXPERIENCE - Posted 12/22/10

URL: http://www.deceptionofdisease.com/?p=149

This is a firsthand account of using Hyperbaric Oxygen Therapy (HBOT) as one of many natural treatments for symptoms of Autism. This particular article recounts our initiation into the therapy. The date was December 22, 2010 and our 10-year old, Danielle, was scheduled for her very first HBOT session.

To be honest, I was a little distracted that day because our 3rd daughter had a minor surgical procedure done that morning. While I was thrilled about having Danielle receive the HBOT for the first time, my efforts and emotions were spent tending to Victoria. That morning while we were on our way home from Victoria's surgery my dad took Danielle to her appointment at the Grass Valley Wellness Center. The founders are dear family friends who have been most instrumental in pointing us toward various methods of healing for our kids. For a few years we've been aware that the Wellness Center offers HBOT, but recently my dad had taken the initiative to get the ball rolling on getting Danielle and Sophia appointments to receive the therapy. We had decided Danielle would go first.

Basically, the entire session took about an hour and my dad was able to sit inside the chamber with her so that she wouldn't be nervous. She was also allowed to take her Nintendo DSi inside to help pass the time. He described it to me once they got home, saying that it felt a lot like when you ascend or descend in elevation or on an airplane. It even sounded a little bit like being in an airplane, and they frequently had to adjust their ears to the pressure. The therapist did mention that if our daughter was congested it could be quite uncomfortable, but she had no problems at all since that was not the case. And once Danielle got used to being inside the chamber she began to relax and play her games.

THE IMMEDIATE RESULTS

I was in a bit of shock and awe over that entire conflict-free day! You see, one of the last major blocks we're facing on Danielle's road to recovery from Autism has been a constant, consistent, persistent, ever-present opposition from her pertaining to almost every activity or request we initiate. I've never had her evaluated for Oppositional Defiant Disorder, but when I take a look at the list of symptoms of ODD I feel like I'm reading a brief description of her life up to now. From as far back as I can remember (once she began to communicate), she has protested against every single thing...even against her own desires! This, of course, is mainly directed toward me or her dad (sometimes my parents too) because she doesn't have to "hold it together" at home or with us like she does when in public (although it often occurs with us in public to a lesser degree).

When she first began to communicate it would go something like this: Let's say Danielle wanted to eat an apple. She would approach me and say with an upset voice, "Mommy, you said I can't have an apple?!" After several minutes of "arguing" the fact that I will gladly give her an apple, she would finally accept it and eat it. Most of the time it would require that I say something like, "OK, Danielle, then I won't give you an apple," and then she would immediately accept it in opposition to the statement. Often the scene involves yelling and anxiety on her part. As she has gotten older and more verbal, the interchanges sometimes become very drawn out. We have taken many hours of parent ABA training classes and just this month wrote a behavioral plan with our consultant in order to try and address the arguing. It has spilled over into her socialization skills as well, making friendships even more difficult than they already were for her to nurture and navigate. She may want nothing more than to see "Sally," talking about it off and on for hours until the moment arrives to see and greet "Sally." At that very moment when she sees "Sally" she acts the exact opposite of what she feels toward Sally - to the point of outright rudeness and mistreatment of "Sally". It seems an evil prison which holds captive her very ability to pursue the simple and beautiful desires of her heart.

I KEPT BRACING MYSELF ALL DAY

Not once that day did I have a single protest, argument, meltdown, or conflict from her of any kind. This is nothing short of AMAZING! Believe me, there were many instances that day when I braced myself for the typical reaction. When I asked her to clean her room I was mentally going over our behavioral plan so that I could be ready to act. When we went to see Christmas lights she wanted to know why we couldn't get outside and walk like everybody else. She calmly accepted my reply and asked, "Can we walk next year?" You could have picked my jaw up off the floor.

Here are the qualities I noticed in her the day of her first HBOT session:

These are qualities we've been targeting in prayer lately so that she can be happier and more content, and so that her friends will not feel alienated by her.

- Ability to go with the flow
- Ability to hear and accept a verbal reply that we provide to a question she may have
- Willingness to calmly follow directions or comply with a request
- Respectfulness
- General sense of happiness
- Greater sense of humor
- Agreeable

- Ability to converse without becoming visibly agitated or angry
- I did not notice her being irritable at all that day

I do believe these results were a direct result of the HBOT session. That evening my mom told me that during the morning, before Danielle and my dad left for the session appointment, the conflicts were pretty bad. I was already beginning to understand why so many families have purchased portable HBOT chambers for their homes.

If you would like to read more about some clinical results of HBOT for Autism, here is another article which explains a 2009 double-blind study.
http://abcnews.go.com/Health/AutismNews/story?id=7070353&tqkw=&tqshow=&page=1

Post #2

ANOTHER MIRACLE OF "SORTS" - HBOT SESSION 2 - Posted 12/31/10

URL: http://www.deceptionofdisease.com/?p=175

We were on Christmas break from school, so we thought we'd take advantage of this time and get the kids back up to The Grass Valley Wellness Center for another Hyperbaric Oxygen

Therapy (HBOT) session. This was Tuesday, December 28th, and this time the plan was to have our second daughter Sophia go as well. It was to be Sophia's first treatment and Danielle's second. The results of Danielle's first session were so astonishingly good that we just couldn't wait to see how Sophia would respond.

Danielle's incredible change in mood and behavior (for the good) lasted about 4 days before she began to show signs of frustration and defiance over small things. But I was not discouraged in the least. I'm well acquainted with the nature of the healing process by now, and I understand that long-term results come with an accumulation of the right kinds of treatments. We were convinced that we were on to something special with this HBOT. And once you strike a vein of gold you just need to keep on following it all the way.

DANIELLE'S FEELINGS ABOUT HBOT
Danielle was quite upset when I explained that she would be going back for another treatment. We waited to tell her until Tuesday when we picked her and Sophia up from a sleepover. She asked what we'd be doing that day, and when she heard the answer she was hardly fit to be around. She yelled and argued about it for the next hour and a half, before having to depart for Grass Valley. When it got down to it, she was able to explain that she didn't like the feeling it produced in her ears (the frequent adjustment of pressure).

Once my dad (and my mom went this time as well) arrived at the Wellness Center with Danielle and Sophia, it was time to get them into the tank. The plan was to have Sophia go inside with Danielle this time, along with their pillows, blankets, and toys. Sophia began to weep and become very anxious about it, to the point that my dad didn't have the heart to force her inside in front of the therapist. (If it had been only family around we all might have made her go in, knowing it would not have harmed her.) Oh well, at least she'd been exposed to the situation and next time would be better prepared. On the other hand, Dad was surprised to watch Danielle go right into the tank without a single protest. He got in with her and as soon as the machine was turned on, she fell fast asleep (thanks to the late night at the sleepover, no doubt).

JAW DROPPING RESULTS FROM SESSION #2
There was an IMMEDIATE change in Danielle's behavior and mood on the hour-long trip home. My mom explained that her attitude and behavior was so negative on the drive up to the center that they kept going only because they knew the prize that was ahead once they reached the destination and accomplished the mission. Now, here is the scene that made my jaw drop this time. I walked into Danielle's room that evening and "caught her" SORTING HER SILLY BANDS BY COLOR. I have never seen her sort anything in her entire life (she's 10). I used to take all the developmental milestones for granted when my kids were babies, but when you have a child who develops at quite a different pace you begin to take note when various milestones are finally met. When she was younger I actually gave up trying to work with her on things like sorting colors because she just seemed not to "get it" and

became frustrated with the activity. There were bigger fish to fry anyway...like potty training, making requests, tolerating minute changes in routine, etc.

I was so excited about this sorting activity that I even had to take a picture of it. To me, it's a sign that something is going on in her neurological pathways.

Again, had no abnormal or irrational conflicts for several days following the 2nd treatment. It was a JOY! I can say without hesitation that it was the very best Christmas holiday we had ever shared with our kids to date. Free of stress and conflict and anxiety. I give all thanks to God and my parents for such a precious gift and significant personal discovery.

POST #3

My First Dive - And First Meaningful Conversation - HBOT Session 3 - Posted 1/10/11

URL: http://www.deceptionofdisease.com/?p=212

Today was the day for Sophia's first time in "the tank" as Danielle calls it. After having 2 HBOT sessions, Danielle is now a veteran, but she still acted grumpy about the whole thing all the way up to Grass Valley. Sophia was going to have no choice in the matter this time, and I was going in to ensure that she was at ease as much as possible. Dad had all her Polly-Pockets gathered together and ready to go along for the ride, but Sophia refused to take them because, "they would be too scared!" Danielle had her Nintendo DSi, I had my mini-cam and Don's iPad, and Sophia would have to be content with no toys.

We arrived at The Grass Valley Wellness Center and I was very pleased to meet Cherie, the manager. We have known the founders for years, but I had not yet personally met Cherie before. We walked back to the HBOT room and were greeted by the "portable" tank. Cherie explained the communication process to me before I got inside.

There are little windows in the top and at each end. She seals you up inside and can then communicate with you through the windows using hand signals. Thumbs up means, "My ears are doing fine." Thumbs down means, "My ears are not doing well." When the hour is up she signals you as well. When she explained that to me I wondered why I would need her to give me a signal at the end of the session.

My dad had already prepared the little bed inside by wrapping it with the sheet we had brought from home. We had pillows at each end and one blanket to share. One person at a time can wear the oxygen mask and in order to avoid freaking Sophia out we had Danielle wear it. That way Sophia could just get an understanding of the entire process. My job was to make sure she didn't feel scared.

FIRST 10 MINUTES OR SO

Danielle wasn't very happy about being back, but willingly got herself settled in without a single protest. At first, she seemed intent on going to sleep and was quite unsociable toward me and Sophia, not allowing me to take photos of her at that point. Sophia and I were simply getting acclimated to the environment. It was a relief to discover the "descent" was not as dramatic as I had anticipated. I've never enjoyed pressure under even 6 feet of water, plus I had a tiny bit of a sinus ache this morning and was praying it wouldn't turn into grave discomfort. It didn't. There were about 3-4 seconds where I felt a tad anxious about being inside of the tank, but it quickly subsided and Sophia and I both began to relax.

DANIELLE'S DISPOSITION CHANGED

Within the first 15 minutes Danielle exuded an overall sense of well-being. She cheered right up and began to joke with us and play games. I could visibly see the change come over her. I think that's why she doesn't protest a bit in getting into the machine. She knows this treatment makes her feel better.

TAKING TURNS

I began to wonder if Sophia would get any physical benefit out of this experience without wearing the oxygen mask. At the half-way point I decided to make Sophia wear it for the remainder of the session. She complained the entire time, but not because it was uncomfortable. She just wouldn't let it go. In the same way that my little sister wouldn't let something go that had happened several hours before (when we were young). I like that Sophia reminds me of my sister sometimes. My sister is one of the people I admire most in the world, so it makes me smile when I see similarities to her in any of my daughters. This particular trait works really well for my sister and all the people she loves because she is so tenacious when she goes after something. You want her praying for you!

THE SIGNIFICANCE OF THE LAST SIGNAL

Remember when I said before how I couldn't figure out why I would need Cherie to let me know the session was over? Well, I found out why that was important right after she gave me the signal. Wow - you come back "up" more quickly than you descend, so you kind of need to be prepared for it. Ha ha. It was actually kind of funny. Danielle was coaching Sophia, reminding her to keep yawning.

RESULTS FROM TODAY - SOPHIA

You know, Sophia has always been a little bit more easy going than Danielle for the most part. But lately she has raised loud and whiny complaints when her sisters try and play Polly-Pockets with her. Tonight, however, she and Victoria played for a very long time without a single argument. I'll keep watching over the next couple of days to see if this was a coincidence or a seemingly actual result of the HBOT. We'll see!

RESULTS FROM TODAY - DANIELLE

Danielle's disposition was, again, much more agreeable. Like I said earlier I noticed a definite change in her inside that tank. And it wasn't just a change in behavior. You know your own kid. You know their energy...their demeanor...their nature. That's where I saw the change.

Another notable thing happened tonight that is so rare I cannot remember the last time it occurred. Danielle and I shared an enjoyable conversation with a meaningful exchange. There was no confusion, no frustration, no agenda. She was making her lunch downstairs and it was a little dark because everyone else in the house had gone to their bedrooms for the night. I went down to get a cup of water and here's how it went down...

Danielle: **"Why did you get such a big cup?"**

Me: **"Because I'm very thirsty!"**

Danielle: **"You could use a smaller cup if you want."** (pleasant, sing-songy voice)

"Mom, did you go to Justice to look at the silly-bands?"

"No."

"How come? You don't like to wear silly bands?"

"Well, they're for kids."

(I decided to stick around...what a window of opportunity...she was interested in conversing! Dare I ask her a question?)

"Danielle, what's your favorite store?"

"Uhh, Target. Mom, did you go to Justice when you were my age?"

"No, there was no Justice when I was your age."

"They didn't build it yet?"

(I was amazed at this reasoning and at her ability to convey the reasoning inside her head.)

"No, they didn't. We didn't have the Roseville Galleria. Only Sunrise Mall."

"Oh... " (...embarrassed look and sweet little smile on her face as she diligently worked on packing her lunch)

"Mom, what do we do now?"

"Well, I like taking to you while you make your lunch."

(More embarrassed smiles from her.)

"Mom, why don't you go upstairs and let me finish making my lunch? I'll see you tomorrow."

She came over and gave me a hug and a kiss. I walked back to my room with a happy heart.

I'll treasure this moment for the rest of my life. I'm believing and proclaiming that it was an amazing start toward more frequent, meaningful conversations. So thankful am I that I'm recording it all here. She's 10 and for the first time we talked back and forth about shopping. Not just a mom trying to pull conversation out of her daughter. But a daughter who was able to express her inward desire to better know her mom. A daughter who was able to pose a meaningful question toward that discovery. A daughter who was not distracted by sensory or auditory processing frustrations in doing so. A daughter who is bravely spreading her wings. Watch out world!

Thank you, Lord!

POST #4

You Gotta Have Faith! - Posted 2/24/11

URL: http://www.deceptionofdisease.com/?p=298

Right now when people meet us for the first time, or if they have only become acquainted with us in the last couple of years, they find it difficult to believe that Danielle and Sophia were ever diagnosed with Autism. However many of you do remember how they were almost completely lost to us, seemingly once and for all. And you can attest to the dramatic turnaround in their abilities, behaviors, and prognosis.

Some would say that the recovery is because of early intervention. Because of ABA therapy. Because of our willingness to adhere to such a strict toxic free and whole food lifestyle over an extended period of time. I'd like to put all of that into perspective because believe me, if these things were the cause of healing there would be a lot more cases of kids coming off of the spectrum on a regular basis. I can only begin to describe the ongoing effort made on the part of parents and educators. If it were something we could all bring about by our own attempts and pursuits or by known regimens then there would be no more epidemic. These things are all good, but they alone do not produce the kind of results we have been blessed to experience. There's another secret component.

Please get this, because if you don't get this then nothing else you are doing for your situation will matter. It will all be for naught. If you don't believe that your kids, your situation, your circumstances will turn around then your efforts are null and void. Every therapy you pursue, every homemade-from-scratch morsel of food you make, every Heavenly promise you declare, must be mixed with faith! You can take every bit of information you find and run with it, but if you're doing it full of fear then all your good work is being cancelled out right in front of your eyes.

I know people who go to great lengths to eat right and exercise with one thought in mind: "I'm afraid to get sick and die. What if I don't live long enough to see _____?" They are full of fear and worry about their future. Maybe you're putting your child into ABA or a Special Ed class with thoughts of "I'm afraid they'll never fit in. I'm afraid they won't be able to ever live independently. What if they never_____?" You're worried about their future all the time. We must resist fear because it's a dream-killer.

YOU MUST UNDERSTAND THIS. During all the hours I spent in the kitchen learning how to make all kinds of new things, I envisioned every cook book, spatula, measuring cup, and ingredient as a powerful weapon in my hands against the child-stealing invader that had entered our lives. Sometimes I would even read healing scriptures aloud as I stirred and cooked. As I rubbed homeopathic flower remedies on the tummies of my girls I did it with faith, choosing to believe that every symptom was being overpowered and ousted out of their bodies. Every time I made a concoction of powdered supplements and juice and had to literally force them to drink it (especially in the beginning), I imagined the toxins being flushed away as faith was attached to every vitamin molecule going into their systems. Even the times when the house was full of stress due to their inability to process their environment (including words, touch, schedule, etc.) — even in those times I remember standing in the middle of it all and consciously making myself just breath and believe…just breath and believe.

Hebrews 4:2b …but the word which they heard did not profit them, not being mixed with faith in those who heard it.

I REMEMBER ONE DAY SO VIVIDLY. It was a Sunday afternoon and for most of my life I had identified Sunday afternoons with rest. Through my growing up years Sunday afternoons were for play dates, naps, or whatever one wanted to do to relax. Anyway, this particular Sunday afternoon was being spent at my parents' house. Don and I were there with Danielle (5), Sophia (3), and infant Victoria. Everyone was trying to relax and I was laying down with Danielle in one of the bedrooms for a little snooze. We were only a couple of months into our intense detox protocol and nutritional plan (better described in the book), but at that point I could see no light at the end of the tunnel. I don't remember now what set her off (very few things didn't set her off back then), but she was in the middle of a meltdown. I broke down crying because I did not know how to help her. I didn't know what to do.

In that moment I had a choice to make. The same choice that had to be made not just every day, but sometimes dozens of times in a single day. I had to choose to believe that things would change! I had to decide that I was going to fan the flame of every hope, dream, and God-given promise for her life. In that moment God loudly spoke a mantra in my heart which I held onto daily for months and years to come.

"What you see with your eyes is irrelevant."

We were trekking slowly up an enormous mountain and I could feel gravity trying to pull us back. We were aware of maybe only two other families that had reached the summit and were not yet all the way down the other side. The mountain was mostly uncharted, the conditions were harsh, and we knew that without God as our guide we would have neither the energy nor the expertise to reach the other side. Was I sad? Yes. Was I unsure about how to handle it? Yes. Was I grief-stricken? All that and more. But in the middle of all those emotions, right there in that bed I let the tears fall and I chose to believe that things would turn around and that we would eventually not only climb the mountain, but also watch it crumble behind us as we moved forward into the future! I had to have faith.

WHAT DO YOU HAVE TO LOSE BY BELIEVING? Many people no longer give themselves permission to hope or believe. The hurt is already so deep that it's tempting to cut your emotional losses and just deal with things as they are. I remember a few months after that Sunday afternoon I was sitting with our amazing in-home ABA therapy coordinator during one of our quarterly reviews, and I declared that my kids would one day be completely symptom free. This was not said with anger, sarcasm, or the grinding of a proverbial ax. I was not on a soapbox. I just felt it very necessary to insert those words of faith into the meeting, in the middle of reviewing otherwise discouraging data. At that time there was absolutely nothing in the earth realm that would have confirmed the possibility of their coming out of autism. The current goals were about helping them tolerate answering or asking a simple 5-word question and the like. I remember feeling the audacity of my remark permeate the room. Although the therapists certainly must not have known what to think about my statement, the atmosphere absolutely changed. May you have the audacity to believe for what you cannot see so that all of your efforts will be mixed with faith.

Romans 14:23b …for whatever is not from faith is sin.

Acknowledgements

This is not the first book I've ever started, but it is the first book I've ever finished. There are so many people to thank, many of whom have no idea how great their impact was or of their contribution to our lives.

First and foremost is Jesus Christ, without whom we would have had no reason or basis for hope of healing or recovery. He alone provides the Way of Life, and He gave everything to purchase the healing and hope that we eagerly and gratefully embrace.

Secondly, our families have been a source of amazing help and support through every difficulty and hardship, as well as every victory and mountain high. To my husband Don, I want to say "Thanks from the bottom or my heart. What we've been through together would have torn many apart, but instead you drew nearer and we became stronger in our faith, hope and love. You freely gave me the time to work on putting our story in writing. I love you!" Also invaluable to the road we have traveled are our parents, Russell & Judy McCollough and Richard and Dixie Proctor, Marc & Angela Milligan (my sister and her husband), Denny Proctor (Don's brother) and Julie Sims (who is my sister from another mother) and numerous other aunts, uncles and cousins. We're a large pack, we are! And we believe in each other.

Thirdly, and very significant is our church family: Impact Church. Abouding gratitude is provoked when I think of their unconditional love and support for us and anyone else who would encounter this amazing group of people. Thank you for your help to us in every possible way.

I'd also like to thank Dr. Lisa Hosbein-Mackenzie and Dan Mackenzie, two of the people God has used to help change the course of our healing journey on more than one occasion.

Finally, words cannot describe the appreciation we have for the village of educators, administrators, therapists, behaviorists, physicians, and babysitters who have been our counselors, comforters and friends.

Contact | Booking

info@deceptionofdisease.com
www.deceptionofdisease.com
www.facebook.com/deceptionofdisease

www.christaproctor.com

Bringing Good News

Made in the USA
San Bernardino, CA
15 May 2013